Bat-Socks, Vegas & Conservative Investing

Bat-Socks, Vegas & Conservative Investing

A simple-to-understand, non-Wall-Street approach to conservative investing

David P. Vick

ISBN 978-1-105-63647-9

For those wishing to learn more about the ABC Planning process, The ABC Model of Investing, and The ABC's of Conservative Investing Workshop, please visit our web site at www.planningwithabc.org.

To Diane and Tom,
Who am I without you?

- Acknowledgements -

While it is hard to thank everyone who has contributed to this effort, I want to acknowledge a few special people that really made the book possible.

First, I want to thank all my client-partners who, over the years, have put their trust in me for their financial needs. We have shared a lot together, both life and death, which tend to be big issues. You have taught me so much and I feel blessed to have known all of you. I know if I tried to list here all the client-friendships I've developed, I would run out of room and still leave someone out, so I won't even try; just know you are all greatly appreciated. I have to mention Sylvio and Lenora; you two have gone far beyond the call of duty, encouraged me greatly, and I treasure our friendship.

Second, as I have trained thousands of agents over the last 10 years, I would be remiss if I didn't thank all of you for what you have taught me. Tom J., Navi D., Chris S., Tom M., Mike L., Steve D., David &Trina S., Rod A., Bill W., Chuck V., Cam D., Patrick W., and so many more; you have trained me well, so thank you very much. I have to also recognize the staff and marketers at Dressander & Associates for putting up with my craziness over the years. Cheryl, you make the whole thing happen daily! Thank you! Tom and Caroline at Baseline, you have been behind the scenes cheering me on and doing your "image" creation thing. Thank you so much. I can't thank my administrator Stefanie Yuen enough for covering for me during my book-writing "disappearances." I have been incredibly blessed by all of you. Mike Dressander, you have made me believe in myself from the very beginning and have an extraordinary ability to make dreams turn into reality. You are an incredible friend, mentor, and dare I say…silly man! Thank you for making this even possible! (Love, Gunner).

The last two are really the first two. Diane and Tom, you have gone way beyond the call of duty to help me write this book. Tom, I really couldn't have done this and I wouldn't have even started it if you didn't forgo a summer job and give your summer to me. You are an incredible young man, gifted in your chosen profession, and no one could have a better son. Our relationship is more than father and son, but you already knew that. I love you beyond words.

Diane, where do I begin? Don't worry, I won't embarrass you in print, (too much). Thank you for your belief in me. You told me years ago I should write and encouraged me in doing so year after year. You have given of yourself tirelessly while putting up with my shenanigans time and time again. You have fought the good fight alongside me and I'm quite certain my clients love you much more than they care about me. I could go on, but you are the love of my life and I'm not afraid to have the world know it. For all you do and who you are, thank you and I love you.

I really do wish my mom and dad could have seen this project, but they passed away in the last year. I am truly a result of their love and belief in me. I miss them terribly, but will see them again I'm sure.

So, that's it. I'm sure I left somebody out….oh yes, the crew at Caribou Coffee in St. Charles, Illinois which has been my secret writing get-away, thank you very much for your "best-in-class" service.

Okay, I'm sure that's it now. Thank you everyone! Oh, and …

- Introduction -

Mashed Potatoes

I can't tell you how many people have asked me what my book is about. Those who are professional writers tell me I should be able to answer that in one sentence. Ha! I have never answered anything in one sentence. I know I'm long winded and love to hear myself talk, but one sentence? Really?

I don't think so.

I remember sitting at the dinner table when I was 5 or maybe 6 years old in Missoula, Montana. We lived in a great old house with a coal room in the basement (a very scary place), with all the bedrooms upstairs. The house was on a corner, had a big apple tree in the back yard, and creaked like an old rocking chair.

Sitting at dinner, stuffing myself with mashed potatoes, fried chicken, and trying hard not to eat my peas, I listened to Mom and Dad talk about their day. I can see them in my mind's eye discussing who knows what. I say that because I don't remember a thing they ever said at that table, only that it sounded important. Most nights I would eat and listen, then...fall asleep. Right at the table with my face planted in the mashed potatoes. I would wake up in my bed wondering how I got there and why my pillow smelled like gravy.

So, why write a book on conservative investing? Simple, I don't like what's out there in the market. It's the same old blah, blah, blah. And it's boring blah at that! It sounds financial, which isn't surprising, but most of it makes me yawn. Although I do love the titles that promise to make you rich in three easy steps, or "How to Pass on Millions to Your Heirs" or "Ten Ways to Blow All Your Money!" It seems there is more fluff than substance and the substance is so boring it makes me fall asleep in my mashed potatoes.

Who's this book for?

I write this book for the age 50 and uppers. Some of them have lost their "uppers," but not lost their senses and want a down-to-earth, easy-to-understand way to look at their finances. I mean do you really understand what your broker is saying? Well, maybe, but I think you could understand a lot more if people would just speak plainly, in terms we all are familiar with. Standard deviation, beta, and means reversion are terms foreign to most, yet are used daily in the planning community.

When I was a youth pastor I used to have to explain deep theological concepts to junior high students. Now that's a challenge! Wall Street jargon is easy in comparison. I believe if a junior high student couldn't understand the concept, then I ought to explain it in such a way as they could, using stories and media to put the concept on their level. If they still didn't get it, I would reword my explanation, tell a few more stories, and keep on trying 'till they got it. The problem is not the junior high student. If you are having a hard time understanding Wall Street, it's not you that's the problem.

I think this book is for those who believe Wall Street "explanations" have become disconnected with Main Street; that Wall Street is a broken culture. I believe Wall Street says one thing and the average person sitting in front of the television says, "Huh?" They are reasonably intelligent people with a lifetime of experiences and are not stupid. Yet, when it comes to finances they're made to feel like bumbling fools in need of a "real professional." Yeah right, someone who will take their money and do what's best for themselves, their company, and everyone else but the investor. The Wall Street philosophy of "Greed is Good" is rampant throughout the financial community.

We live in crazy times—upside-down times when all the price tags in the store seemed to have been changed overnight and no one has noticed. Where a pair of socks has the price tag of a video camera and a suitcase the tag of a q-tip. Our values are out of whack. We pay a guy who can shoot a basketball through a hoop millions of dollars, while a social worker who is in the trenches changing lives day in and day out struggles to pay the electric bill and wonders, "why?"

These values are ever present in the Wall Street community and that is what I mean by the culture being broken. If the center of the financial universe is Wall Street and that culture's values are broken, then those who listen to Wall Street's advice are in serious trouble.

We need a new voice. A new way to understand how to invest that makes sense to conservative investors, literally millions of those approaching and already in retirement who are depending on sound financial counsel to live out their retirement.

That is why I wrote this book. Wall Street is a broken, disconnected culture and the average conservative investor needs a financial plan that makes sense. Mom and Dad used to call it common sense. I don't think Wall Street knows that term.

So, my hope is that you'll have a little fun reading my stories and maybe, just maybe, you will begin to understand that the concepts involved in making your retirement a success are not out of your reach the way so much was out of my reach at the dinner table so long ago. On the other hand, you might continue to listen to Wall Street's blah, blah, blah and let the money you saved all your life fall asleep in your mashed potatoes. I'll leave it up to you.

Pass the gravy please.

- Contents-

Appendixes

- One -

Bat-Socks & Vegas

My brother Bob was the coolest kid growing up—well, at least in my opinion. He was one of two older brothers and one younger. Bob was three years older and I thought he was on the cutting edge of almost everything. He colored life inside the lines and was choosy when it came to fads. Growing up in Missoula, Montana during the 60s wasn't exactly the center of the Hippy movement, so our choices on fads were limited and probably a year behind by the time they got to us.

Bob really got into the *Batman* TV series when it came out. You remember? Adam West as Batman, along with Robin, the Joker, and of course Cat Woman. Bob loved Batman. Every kid loved Batman, but not every kid took a black felt marker and drew the Bat symbol on his white socks. Bob did, and he wore those "bat-socks" with pride, for a few months at least. Then he was on to a different fad. Girls maybe. I just remember going into his dresser, finding those socks and wearing them when he wasn't home. I think I wore holes in them. Then one day they were gone. Weird.

That's a fad for you. In fashion one day, and in the garbage the next.

Conservative investing is not like wearing Bat-socks. It's not a fad. It's not something you do for a few months and then try the next mutual fund flavor of the month. Conservative investing is core investing. Its long-haul investing.

There is a basic need for those who use this strategy, which is simply the need to sleep at night. They don't want to worry about losing money. They are not after quick market gains and fast money schemes. To understand a conservative investor's mindset, you need to understand the concept of "risk" and the role it plays in investing.

Define risk?

Vegas. We're done. Next?

The investing community thinks in terms of "risk aversion" when it comes to assessing a person's "risk tolerance." It's funny, but you know what I think of? VEGAS, baby! It's the center of the universe when it comes to risk.

When people go to Vegas, they fly into an ocean of risk. You can lose so much in Vegas, and I'm not just talking about money. The potential to win—and win big—is what lures millions upon millions of people. What's strange is Vegas is filled with conservative investing retirees who go there to gamble their retirement savings on the "BIG WIN."

In reality, people go to Vegas for the shows, endless buffets, and to lose a "certain amount of money." This is money they actually budgeted and predetermined to lose. When they win and come home with more than they planned to lose, they are just plain giggly. However, when they lose their budgeted gambling money, they are still happy. They expected to lose a budgeted amount and have fun watching Cirque du Soleil and gaining ten pounds. When they lose more than the budget, they are upset. It wasn't what they expected. Not only did they gain ten pounds, they couldn't manage their money! And that's just plain discouraging! Yet, that's the effect gambling has on us. It's fun until you lose more than you thought you would and are mad at yourself for not sticking to your guns…and your budget. It's called discipline.

That's a conservative mindset, a disciplined mindset. When you lose, you get upset because you weren't in control. The degree of your "upset-ness" is the degree of your conservative nature.

Wall Street, however, disconnects with Main Street by defining risk as "the chance that your actual return will be different than what you expected."(1) In other words, they define risk as the potential for your assets to gain *or* lose.

Conservative investors laugh at the thought of gaining money as a risk. Instead a conservative investor defines risk as the potential to lose money. It's not a matter of return on your principal, but return of your principal. A conservative investor's aversion to risk, then, is how they feel about losing more than they expected.

Risk vs. Reward

One of the fundamental ideas in finance is the concept of risk vs. reward. It is generally assumed that the greater the risk, the greater the potential return. For instance, a U.S. Treasury bond pays out less of a return than a corporate bond because the U.S. Government is less likely to go bankrupt than a corporation. Most advisors will tell you both the Treasury bond and corporate bond can be conservative investments. Yet, the risk associated with the corporate bond pushes the issuer of that bond to offer a higher return.

If risk is the chance that the outcome will be negative, a conservative investor wants as little of it as possible. They want to protect principal, protect against inflation, provide income or the potential for income, and increase the value of their portfolio.

There are many types of risk. Here's a short list:

- Market risk
- Business risk
- Purchasing power risk (inflation)
- Sovereign risk
- Interest rate risk
- Reinvestment risk
- Liquidity risk
- Country risk
- Systematic risk
- Unsystematic risk
- Event risk
- Political risk
- Price risk

If reading through this list starts to make your blood pressure go up and your skin turn clammy, you are definitely a conservative investor. I'm guessing you already knew that. Below is a standard Risk Aversion Scale. If you wanted to discover where you fit on the scale, you could take a Risk Assessment Questionnaire offered by various investment companies. (You can check out a sample "Risk Assessment Questionnaire" in Appendix Three.)

Risk Tolerance Scale

Conservative Moderate Aggressive

Basically, how you feel about an adverse affect in your portfolio is your personal Risk Tolerance. For instance, let's say you experienced losses in 2000-2003 and again in 2008, but only to the degree at which the broad market suffered losses. You felt bad, yet you may have also believed your assets would recover over time, so you didn't lose any sleep over it. If that was true about you, you are at least a "moderate" on the scale.

On the other hand, imagine you are talking to a friend who had experienced the same losses as above. If you begin to get a pit in your stomach, your palms get all sweaty and you can't avoid the feeling of complete devastation even though it isn't even your money, you are definitely a "conservative" on the Risk Tolerance Scale. You are a conservative investor. When it comes down to 'messin' with your assets, this ain't Vegas, baby. Right?

How to be a Conservative Investor: Life in the "Slow Lane"

If risk avoidance is your heartbeat, then you have to realize patience is the key to conservative investing. Not patience in the sense of recovering from losses, but patience in accruing gains over a longer period of time. Lower risk assets typically are the tortoise, not the hare. While there have been times in history when fixed assets have had high yields, it isn't the norm.

My Aunt Ginny gave me a copy of my great grandfather's handwritten history of the family's American adventure. He tells of his parents coming over on the boat in 1835 and settling in West Virginia. They pulled up roots and joined a wagon train out to Kansas where they lived in sod huts and burned Buffalo chips in the winter to stay warm. While in Kansas, my great grandfather's family tried farming and started a rope manufacturing business that eventually failed, causing them to abandon their luxurious huts and headed north. Traveling through Utah, he mentions meeting a helpful Mormon family and moving on to Idaho. In the mid 1880's, they homesteaded a 160-acre farm outside Boise and settled down once again. Working as cattle herders, the family became deeply in debt as they tried to make the homestead work. He talks about a lot of issues during those days, including blizzards, illness, and incredibly hard, lonely work. One of the worries that kept his father awake at night was the interest on the debt…18%! I was amazed he remembered that detail 70 years later as he wrote the story.

I was also interested in what he called, "Cleveland Badges." It seems that in the 1890's, while Grover Cleveland was in his second term as President of the United States, the economy was in a severe recession following the Panic of 1893. The "badges" mentioned were actually patches on their clothing. They were so poor and times were so bad they couldn't afford to buy new clothes. They just patched the ones they had, blaming it on the President. Thus the term, "Cleveland Badges."

I tell you this story because it illustrates how high interest rates were back in the 1890's and it wasn't until the late 1970's and early 80's that interest rates were that high again, along with double-digit inflation. High interest rates seem to cycle through history over longer periods of time. If you are waiting for high interest rates, you are going to have a nice relaxing wait. The truth is that 6-month CD rates from 2000 through 2009 have had a high around 7% and a low of something under 1%. (2)

People using an interest rate strategy make good use of bank deposits, money markets, U.S. Treasuries, and fixed-income assets. For the most part, these assets provide relative security of principal, yet lower returns. The real problem is the loss of purchasing power due to high inflation, which often accompanies times of elevated interest rates.

Benefits of Conservative Investing: Who would want to go through this?

The major league benefit to the ultra-conservative investor who doesn't risk principal is simple: sleep. That's right. They don't worry about their assets when the DOW drops 300 points in a day. They wonder how that poor sucker with his money in the market is doing, and silently gloat.

So then, what is conservative investing and how do you go about it? Simply put, conservative investing is a long-term strategy to manage risk in such a way as to conserve principal while maintaining buying power. What are lower-risk assets? Well, they could be anything.

The real question is, "how do you manage risk?"

It's the subject of the rest of this book, so leave your Bat-socks in the drawer, forget about VEGAS, and dig in.

- Two -

What the Heck Just Happened?

A Crumpled Freshman Mass of Goo

I remember my freshman year in college at the University of Hawaii. I was on a football scholarship coming off a very successful high school career. It wasn't too hard because I was the biggest guy on the team at 6'2" and about 225lbs. I know, that's not so big these days, but back then in Lynnwood, Washington it was large. I had okay speed, played offensive tackle and middle linebacker. I loved playing linebacker. It was the glory position where you get to hit just about anything that moves and have a lot of fun doing it. We had an undefeated team my senior year and I was the Team Co-Captain along with the quarterback Mark Hobbs.

Going to Hawaii, I wanted to quickly work my way to the starting linebacker position and make the traveling squad. If I did that, I would be able to join the team as it traveled back to my home town to play the University of Washington in front of all my friends. Boy, was I really going to impress them. But, something happened. I got to the practice field and the speed of the game was so much faster in college it was hard for me to see what was happening. I remember a Saturday scrimmage about two weeks into "three-a-day" practices in August of 1973 when I realized something had changed.

We had a USC transfer tailback and two flying mountains they called offensive guards. I think they kept these animals in the basement and didn't feed them until after practice. They were mean, ugly…and very fast. When I was put in as middle linebacker against the first team offense, they ran a toss sweep with their stud tailback. I saw the movement go to my left and I ran as fast as I could to the outside and sure enough Igor and his buddy Frankenstein were flying around the outside to block. Now, in high school, being bigger than most, I would simply run over the guards to get to the tailback. So, I gave it a shot.

Igor and Frankenstein didn't even break stride as they ran over me. They left cleat marks on the front of my bloodied jersey as I lay on my back, barely able to breathe. Something was different here and—call me a little slow—but the speed of the college game was so much faster, the players so much larger, I really had an adjustment to make. The game had changed and I was left in a crumpled freshman mass of goo on the turf. I asked myself, "What the heck just happened?"

By the way, this is not a question you want to be asking about your finances at any point in time if you are a conservative investor.

Big Words

I'm generally not a fan of big, $64 words. You know the type, more than two syllables and hard to pronounce. People use them to sound impressive and well educated. Brokers and agents use them for the same reason, but also use them to hide what they may not know. Weird, huh? They use a word they may not completely understand, hoping the person sitting in front of them has no idea what they're talking about, all the while pretending they know what it means. Next time a financial planner uses a term like "standard deviation," ask him to explain it so you can understand. Financial planning should not be that difficult.

I kind of like the word "paradigm," though. I know it goes against my usual tastes, but it sounds so good. I was teaching a Sunday School class one day and used it. I was very proud of myself for sounding so educated. Yet, after I used the phrase "paradigm shift" the class reacted a little odd. They laughed. Imagine that. They laughed at the phrase "paradigm shift." I couldn't understand it so I chuckled and continued the lesson. An older gentleman came up afterward and took me aside, telling me he loved the class and got a lot out of it. He informed me however I had missed pronounced the word. The rest of the class probably thought I did it on purpose, but this wise old gentleman caught it. Paradigm is pronounced "para – dime" not "par – i – di – gum." I can't tell you how many times I had missed pronounced the word in seminars and agent classes I've taught. Using it sounded so intelligent, all the while I sounded like a buffoon.

Just a thought about using big words; make sure you pronounce them correctly. They can make you look like the idiot you decidedly are if you don't! Humor me though, as I try to explain how paradigm shifts have changed for conservative investing. *(You can pronounce it any way you want. No one will know because you're only reading it!)*

Perspective & Paradigm Shifts

What is a paradigm shift? You can think of it as a sort of transformation, a changing of one way of thinking to another. Some might even call it a revolution or a metamorphosis.

In 1610, Galileo stunned the world. While studying the solar system through his telescope, he came to believe Earth orbited the Sun rather than the prevailing worldview of the Sun and planets revolving around the Earth. He was the catalyst for a hard-fought change in how we view the universe.

No one can argue the creation of television was a major change agent in American society. From *Ozzie & Harriett, Gilligan's Island*, Network News, Cable News, ESPN, Fox News, reality TV, shopping channels, to HDTV, television has changed our lives. The constant programming and commercial messages have transformed how we view ourselves and the world around us. Metamorphosis.

The rise of the internet has created a whole new way for people to develop relationships. What an incredible cultural turn in relational development. With MySpace, Facebook, Twitter, eHarmony, and more, the power of the internet to connect people is changing the way we think about who we are, and how we relate to friends, business partners, and love interests. That's pure revolution!

There are also very interesting alterations in "investing paradigms" which have taken place over the last 30 to 40 years. Changes of this magnitude usually take a long time to blossom. I believe our perspective on investing has changed because of a cultural transformation in America and the effect of bear markets—especially big bear markets—on future economies. Let me illustrate.

Looking Back at the Dow from 1980

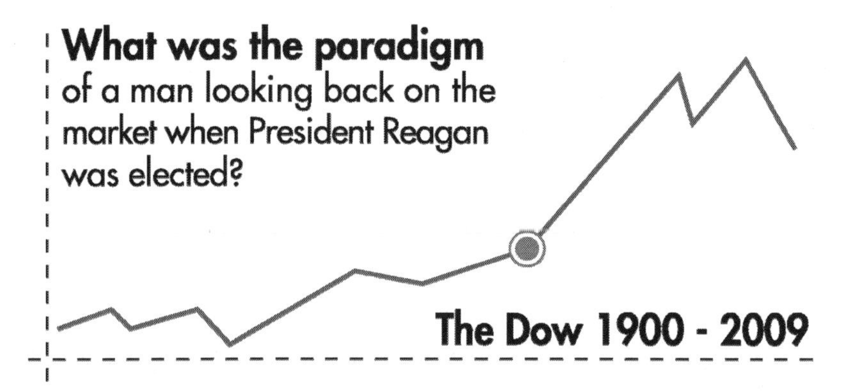

I was talking on the phone with Greg Anderson, a financial planner friend of mine from Colorado. He is a creative sort who has some unique takes on investing. Greg challenged me to look at the last 30 years of investing history in a new light.

You remember the 1970's, don't you? Watergate and Nixon. The Beatles broke up and the Eagles soared. The Village People and YMCA. Presidents Gerald Ford and Jimmy Carter. All the *Airport* movies! Strange years, but they were the prelude to Ronald Reagan and "trickle-down economics."

If you were an investor in 1980, when President Ronald Reagan was elected, what did you see? I mean, if you could literally stand on a time line of the DOW in 1980 and peer backward over the last ten to twenty years, what would you see that would affect how you invested going forward? The 70's were turbulent financial years with investors largely investing in bonds, large cap mutual funds, and blue chip stocks. The 70's were the up and down years of a mid-term bear market that started in the fall of 1965 and didn't recover until the fall of 1982, covering 17 restless years. Who can forget long gas lines and double-digit inflation? That's what you saw looking back from 1980.

Investors in those years believed in the long haul of blue chip investing. Speculation was not a prevalent strategy in the 70's. With the advent of IRAs in the 70's, the average person began to invest more in the market. The beginning of the decade saw an average of 10 million trades in the DOW per day. By the end of the decade, it had increased 5 times to an average of 50 million trades per day and growing. Today, the DOW ranges from about 4 to 10 billion trades per day, mostly made possible by advances in the internet.(1) The speed at which markets change is the speed of information, and information is accelerating geometrically!

The prevalent investor strategy at the beginning of the 80's was unmistakably conservative. They looked for safety and dividends. They weren't "speculative" in nature, but desired small, consistent gains along with dividends. Not much risk.

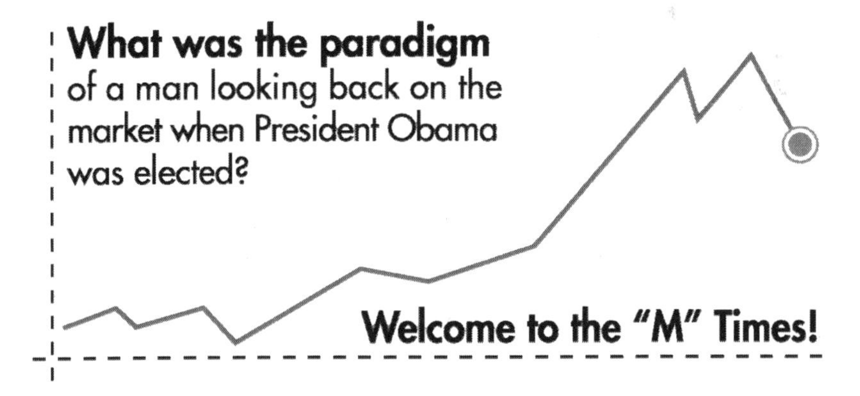

In contrast, what was the view of an investor looking back on the market when President Obama took office in 2009? Again, if you could stand on a DOW timeline and look back, what would you see? My friend Greg titled this the "M-

Generation." Very creative I thought. Yet, I liked the "M-times" a little better. Sounded almost Apocalyptic.

An investor looking back on the last 20 years in the DOW would see a huge M in the graph the closer it got to his time—the "irrational exuberance" of the 1990's Bull market, followed by a tech bubble bursting into a near 50% loss from 2000-2002, followed by a 5-year Dow run up with the peak of the second half of the "M" in October of 2007, followed by the housing bubble, bank bubble, finance bubble, and whatever other bubble was out there, bursting into flames by the low point of March 2009.

My take on Greg's M-Times is that people react in two ways. First, some are numb from the terrifying roller coaster rides and leave their money in the market not knowing what to do but hoping it will come back. It's called Buy and Hope, which we'll discuss later. Second, others are cashing out and are investing in low-interest-rate CD's, money markets, and savings accounts. There is a ton of money on the sidelines. Mass confusion reigns.

Obviously, significant Bear markets cause a change in the way people invest, leaving them asking, "What the heck just happened?"

Gambling vs. Investing: A New Paradigm Shift

Let's take a look at another cultural shift which has taken place over the last 30 years. The cultural trend toward the acceptance of gambling and its influence on our investment styles is truly fascinating. I believe that our perspective on investing has changed because American culture changed first.

Miriam-Webster's online dictionary provides the following definition of investing:

"In·vest" verb

1. *to commit (money) in order to earn a financial return.(2)*

It seems that the word invest almost implies that your principal will be secure and you would receive a gain in addition to your principal. Has a ring of safety, doesn't it? Now let's look at Webster's definition of gambling.

"gam· ble" verb

1. a: to play a game for money or property b: to bet on an uncertain outcome 2: to stake something on a contingency: take a chance (3)

When we look at the dictionary definition of gamble, we see it is more in line with what our investing culture has come to accept over the last 30 years. This point is brought out clearly in a book titled *Blind Faith* by Edward Winslow, 2003. In his book, Winslow presents a dramatic case for the change in investing brought on by the cultural acceptance of gambling, which has increased forty fold over three decades. (4) Take a look at the facts on Gambling:

- Gambling is a $90 billion a year industry.
- 1988— only legal in Nevada and New Jersey.
- 1994 – Operating in 23 states.
- 2000 – Over 34 million people visited Las Vegas.
- 2000 – Over 127 million in casinos nationally.
- 2003 – Operating in 48 states
- Industry take - $750 per participant or $250 per person in U.S. (5)

Do you remember what society thought of gambling in the 1950's, 60's, and 70's? Gambling was considered a negative social element and looked upon with distaste. I'm sure it was one of the seven major sins, and with the exception of sex, I can't even tell you what the other six were (not because my mind stops at the word sex, though). If we look over the last 30 years, gambling has gone from a blight on society, equal to smoking, drinking, pre-marital sex and extra-marital affairs, to a cultural norm. What the heck just happened?

If you've been to Vegas in the last 10 years, you surely can't miss the fact it is a retiree's haven. The very people who, when they were growing up, thought of gambling as evil, have now made Risk City their number one travel destination. Not only that, but some of the most popular cable TV shows are televised gambling events. You can watch it on television and play it online 24 hours a day. It is in our 21st century American blood. The acceptance of gambling represents a definite cultural shift and has doubtlessly had an effect on not only the way we invest, but if we invest at all!

Strangely enough, in 1978 Congress enacted a change in the tax code which enabled much of the change to speculation in our investing culture. They amended Section 401(k). It took effect in 1980, and by 1983 more than half of large companies were setting up 401k plans, a little more than 17,000.(6) Half way through the 1980's, there were less than 8 million people investing in 401ks with about $100 billion invested. By 2006, there were seventy million participants and more than $3 trillion invested.(7) The average American in the 70's wasn't invested in the market, and by 2006 it's a cultural norm. They went from saving in banks to investing in mutual funds just because of the availability? No. There has to be a correlation between our society's acceptance of gambling and the radical flight from safety to speculation. Again, what the heck just happened?

Webster says gambling is wagering money or assets on an uncertain outcome. Tell me the difference between an employee "investing" in an uncertain mutual fund market at one of the most turbulent times in our nation's economic history and "gambling." Please, somebody tell me!

Wait, there's more…

In 1884 Charles Dow began publishing his "Dow Jones Averages" in the *Customer's Afternoon Letter,* which was the forerunner of *The Wall Street Journal*. In 1896, he changed the name to the *Dow Jones Industrial Average,* which consisted of twelve industrial stocks, a departure from the original nine railroad stocks, and two industrial stocks. The first index containing the "Rails," as people referred to it, continued to rival the industrial average's for the next 20 years.(8)

Russell Napier, in his book *The Anatomy of a Bear* tells us these two main indexes, the Dow Jones Industrials and the "Rails" Stock index, were the two main indexes at the turn of the 1900's. During the hard financial times from 1900-1914 and the start of World War I, Napier tells us that the government nationalized the railroads, and guess what happened to that stock index. Right, it virtually went away when the government devalued the rail stocks by their takeover.(9) That was a huge alteration in the market.

Another event that caused a deviation in the market was the creation of the Federal Reserve in 1914. The Fed was created to make our currency "elastic."(10) In other words, to "inflate" the money supply during a recession or depression, the fed would print more money tied very loosely to the gold standard hoping it would grow the economy. That created incredible changes in the financial markets coming out of 1921.

So, what similarities are there to the government involvement during and after the crash of 2008? How about the near nationalization of our banks, auto industry, and most of the 20% of our economy represented in the health care system for starters? And, what changes will these make in economy, stock market, and investing culture?

If you don't know the answer to these questions, then is it wise to have a large portion of your retirement assets in the market? How confident can you be with no protections, or without a strategy to minimize your losses? Large paradigm shifts in the market created by cultural changes and Bear markets is no place to find solid ground.

I'm not saying you should be out of the market during times such as these, but you should have a solid plan to manage risk in accordance with your conservative tolerance. Remember, the question is not "how much money you should have in a mutual fund," but "how do you manage risk?" If you don't have a good enough answer, then your assets along with your retirement future might end up like my football career at Hawaii: a bloodied, crumpled mass of financial goo and you'll be asking, "What the heck happened?"

- Three -

Santa & Six Wall Street Myths

Twas the Night Before Christmas

Santa Claus. The Tooth Fairy. Hercules. Like most kids, I believed in all of these as I was growing up. I actually believed in Santa Claus until I was 11 or 12 years old. I loved Santa. If I was good, he brought me toys. If I was bad, well…let's not go there. My family loved perpetuating this belief, including my two older brothers. They went to great lengths each year to make me believe Santa delivered the presents under our tree on Christmas Eve. You see, each Christmas Eve our family would pile in the car and drive around town to look at Christmas lights. Impossible as it may seem, Santa would know we were out of the house and he placed all the presents beneath the tree by the time we returned.

Before we left the house each year, my mother would be the last one out of the house. I was in the car with my brothers waiting not-so-patiently to get on the road so we could hurry up and return for the presents. Dad would send one of my older brothers in to get mom and he would take forever to come out. Once we got on the road, my Dad would even drop back by the house, go up to our front window and look in. He would shake his head meaning Santa hadn't come yet. Imagine the emotions running through my body. He's here, he's not here, he's here, he's…I'd be deflated. Off we would go again.

As we would drive around the neighborhoods, my Dad and brothers would slyly say, "Look, there he is," or "He's over here" or "He's right above the CAR!" I would frantically try to peer out the side of the car they were pointing to. I never saw him, although sometimes I would say I saw him so I wouldn't be the only one in the car who wouldn't have seen him. It made sense to me back then. What can I say, I had a troubled childhood.

Finally, we would get back to the house, and Dad would check the window again. This time he would send me to check it out. I would scramble to the window take one look and start jumping up and down with excitement. "He came! He came!" I would burst through the front door and see an amazing array of boxes and bows under the tree. I nearly wet myself. How did Santa do it?

My brothers must have loved it year after year wondering how long they could keep it going. It makes you wonder if they did it out of love or some other more sinister motive. Of course when my younger brother Tim was old enough, I continued the tradition. I loved seeing his face light up when he saw those gifts through the window, and also loved that I knew the secret truth.

The truth is Santa was a myth. I know it may come as a surprise to some, but he is definitely a myth. Yes, I know Santa embodies giving, goodness, generosity, and many more positive attributes. Yet, in the end, he's still a myth.

Wall Street Myth or Maxim?

One way Webster's dictionary defines myth is by describing it as a popular belief that has come about by "an unfounded or false notion." Maxim on the other hand, is defined by Webster's as a general truth, or a fundamental principle. Let's take a look at six Wall Street sayings, that many would call maxims. We may in the end, however, find out they are indeed myths. I'll let you decide.

Wall Street Saying #1: "I haven't lost until I sell"

This Wall Street saying actually comes from a reality in the world of taxes. If you bought a stock for $10 a share, and four years later it's worth $20 a share, you have good news. You made money. If you sell the asset at this point, you will have a gain to report on your taxes of $10 a share. You have "realized" your gain. You also have some bad news, a tax due on the gain. This is called a "capital gains tax," which is a tax on the gain in the asset. You are only taxed if you sell the asset, thus you "realize" the gain only by selling the asset.

If however, the share price went down to $5 a share, you have lost money in your investment, and if you sell, you will "realize" a loss. You can use that loss on your tax return to wipe out certain gains. You would not be able to use this to your advantage on your tax returns, unless you sold. In reality, you haven't lost until you sell, is only true when it comes to taxes. It is not true when it comes to investing.

People come to my office every week, bringing in their statements for me to evaluate. As I analyze them, I began to see gains and losses in assets as discussed above. I look at the dollar figure on the statement and it may say they have $500,000 worth of assets. The statement puts dollar figures on assets for people to see how much money there assets are worth. The dollar figure tells you how much money you have in the account.

Sometimes I look at their statement from the previous month and they might have had $600,000 worth of assets. When I asked them how much money they have, they tell me they have $500,000. When I point out that they have lost $100,000, they look at me a little conflicted. They know their statement says they lost the money, but they are trained to believe "I haven't sold it yet so I really haven't lost."

How can this be true? They have exactly how much money is represented on their statement. If they needed cash today they would have $500,000. In the real world, the dollar amount listed on their statement is what they have. In what other area of finance would they ever look at a statement so specific in totals and not believe it. Instead, they believe their broker, who doesn't want to lose the account. He's perpetuating the lie, telling them "you haven't lost because you haven't sold."

People will often want to believe a lie because the truth is too painful to live with. They are in total disbelief of the realities communicated in their statement. The same broker, however, will call them when their assets have grown in value bragging, "See how much money I've made you? Don't you want to invest more?"

When you think about it, if you received a statement from your utility company showing a large increase over your previous month, wouldn't you believe the statement? Surely you wouldn't pay the same amount as last month? Wouldn't you believe what's written in black and white? You might think they made a mistake and call to clarify, yet you would eventually come to an understanding with the utility company on the exact amount you owed.

How can this double standard be true? It's NOT! The old saying, "I haven't lost until I sell," is actually Wall Street manipulating our thinking into believing we didn't lose anything when we actually did. This is a lie spawned from a broken culture bent on deceiving you for their advantage.

If "I haven't lost until I sold" is true, then all bad mortgages would just be a paper loss and the black abyss of 2008 would never have happened. The mindset that an actual loss of value in any asset is only a "paper loss" is the way creative accounting starts. There are no paper losses when it comes to investing. There is only lost money. Sure, you can write it off your taxes, but that is my point exactly. It's a tax reality. For investors, we can't afford to be unrealistic in our outlook, especially in our beliefs about money. We can't afford to take a soft passing glance at our statements and believe a convenient lie.

We have to take a hard look at our statements. We have to tell ourselves the truth. "You haven't lost until you sell" and "it's only a paper loss" is akin to believing Santa really lives. If your broker wants you to keep believing a myth and take you for *another ride around the block,* I urge you to believe what your statement tells you. If you have $500,000 on your statement, please, believe what's written in black and white. You only have $500,000.

The truth is the market goes up and down. Your accounts may very well recover to their old levels, but until then, "you have what you have" is a better catch phrase to use. Reality is always a better place to begin when evaluating how to move forward. You can even say that you have lost money in your investments and if you keep them they may one day regain their value. I'm sure that's what the owners of Enron stock said.

"I haven't lost until I sell" and Santa Claus—Myth or Maxim? You decide.

Wall Street Saying #2: "The large wire houses are the best place to get professional advice."

> *A long time ago, a visitor from out of town came to a tour in Manhattan. At the end of the tour, they took him to the financial district. When they arrived to Battery Park, the guide showed him some nice yachts anchoring there, and said, "Here are the yachts of our bankers and stockbrokers."*
> *"And where are the yachts of the investors?" asked the naive visitor. (1)*

While I don't want to seem jaded, you have to at least acknowledge that something is wrong here. This little story illustrates a common perception in the country that brokers make a lot of money on the backs of their investors. You may agree or disagree, but it is definitely a perception and we are often told that perception and reality are not far apart.

In case you are unsure what a "wire house" is, it is a large brokerage firm with many branch offices and brokers. The branch offices operate under the jurisdiction of the main firm, share financial information and research through a common computer system. Past large wirehouse firms which you might be familiar with are Merrill Lynch, Morgan Stanley, Goldman Sachs, Wells Fargo, or Wachovia. Since 2008, it has gotten a little hard to keep up with these firms because of the meltdowns and mergers.

Many investors are attracted to the big names because they want the comfort of doing business with a large, well known firm. After all, what could go wrong? If the events of 2008 and beyond have not shaken the confidence of the American public in that philosophy, I'm not sure what would.

When major firms file bankruptcy like Lehman Brothers, or are bought out before they fail like Bear Stearns, or when Goldman Sachs is investigated by the government for what is at least considered questionable conduct, you have to wonder if the advice you receive is in *your* best interest.

Not only that, but brokers are reportedly leaving Wall Street firms in droves. After 2008 and 2009, brokers began to consider the possibility that large wire house firms might be more of a liability than a benefit to their careers. The independent advisor used to be looked on as a second-class option for those seeking financial advice. However, many brokers who are leaving the failed large wire houses are going independent. (2) Clearly, they see the need to disassociate themselves with the Wall Street muck being exposed in the daily news.

In typical Wall Street fashion, these firms were selling stocks, proprietary mutual funds and IPOs to their clients who believed they were receiving unbiased advice. The reality is, they were being sold products which best suited the firm's bottom line rather than bettering the client's positions. Their fiduciary responsibility was in question, and the public began to realize it. Lawsuit after lawsuit began to show a broken culture's motivations were highly suspect.

In addition, if you only go to the large wire houses for advice, then you leave out the largest group of advisors who happen to be independent. Most of these advisors are highly qualified professionals with the client's best interests at heart. They don't want any part of a large company telling them what they have to "sell" their clients. They are independent insurance agents, Registered Investment Advisors, and brokers with smaller independent firms concentrating on the needs of individuals as a priority.

Yes, I am biased. I am an independent advisor and train advisors nationally. They are an incredible group of men and women with high integrity, skills, and passion for what they do. Sure, there are bad apples in every barrel, but my experience with advisors across the country is incredibly positive. They work long, hard hours serving their clients and the majority of these exceptional men and women don't own yachts. Their motto is not "Greed is Good," but "People First, Money Second."

So, with brokers leaving large wire houses in great numbers, receiving financial advice from a failing, "out-of-touch with reality system" seems equally questionable. If those giving the advice are leaving, why would you want to stay?

Large wire houses are the best place to get professional advice, Myth or Maxim? You decide.

Wall Street Saying #3: "A diversified portfolio of stocks, bonds, and mutual funds are safe over the long haul."

> *"Wide diversification is only required when investors do not understand what they are doing."* Warren Buffett (3)

My question is simple. If you don't have a clue what you are doing, what are you doing in the market in the first place? An even better question may be, "Does diversification actually provide the safety a conservative investor really desires?"

I was with a bunch of advisors from around the country recently and told them the industry uses the word "diversification" like pixie dust. They laughed of course, because they know it's true. All you have to do is tell a client you are putting an asset in a portfolio to add a little "diversification" and the client will shake their head in agreement. It's really weird! After all, who can argue with "diversification?" Just throw it on anything and people will agree with you.

"Sir, would you like your office furniture to be diversified?"

"Ma'am, are you looking for a little diversification in your wardrobe?"

See? People are trained to agree with you. You can't go wrong with offering diversification.

The only people this doesn't work on are children. They haven't been trained yet by Wall Street. Children don't care about "toy diversification." They just want more toys. I guarantee you one day they will be equally enchanted, because Wall Street has some powerful media mo-jo.

Okay, enough fun. What is the theory behind the pixie dust? Basically, diversification implies you can reduce your overall risk by investing in assets which move in different directions over time and in response to market conditions. You might buy individual stocks and bonds, large cap and small cap, domestic and foreign, financial sector and manufacturing sectors, hoping that if one asset class goes south the other area will go north. This has been the practice for Wall Street firms for decades, based on years of studies.

In an editorial for Investment Advisor Magazine, July 2009 an advisor, commenting on the market collapse in 2008 and 2009, makes the point that Wall Street was broken (again!) and the diversification models used by wealth management advisors failed their largest test ever. The author suggests the following reason:

> *"What went wrong? The fixed income substitutes pushed by the major investment houses" low volatility hedge funds, preferred stocks, asset-backed securities or other structured products, closed-end bond funds, income/mortgage REITs, and master limited partnerships weren't fixed income substitutes at all. None of them is a substitute for the most important characteristic that investors should be looking for from the fixed income portion of their portfolios: safety of principal." (4)*

The editorial goes on to imply that bonds are the only fixed-income asset that should be used to balance risk in portfolios for investors seeking a safe diversification. The problem with bonds, which we'll discuss in a later chapter, is they can also lose money. If you held Bear Stearns bonds, or Lehman Brothers bonds, or if you currently hold California municipal bonds, you may very well have experienced losses or soon will. At the very least, you are or were very nervous.

I can't even imagine how a hedge fund or a preferred stock could be listed as a fixed income asset. Yet, this is exactly what happened to wire house clients. That is why Wall Street is a broken culture. They just don't get it.

In the end, conservative investors in or approaching retirement got sacked in 2008. They just can't afford to lose because their investment horizon is shortened. Sure diversification in a portfolio might lower volatility over the "long haul" of 50 years. When you have to draw income now and make it last for 30 years, you can't afford a broken Wall Street approach.

A diversified portfolio of stocks, bonds, and mutual funds are safe over the long haul, Myth or Maxim? You decide.

Wall Street Saying #4: "Buy & Hold is an Effective Conservative Strategy."

"Buy and hold as a strategy is very questionable…It's worked in the past, but in time of severe market stress it just doesn't work."
Ben Stein, author, lawyer, actor, and financial commentator (5)

Mr. Stein is certainly not THE authoritative voice for financial matters, but I think he says here what many advisors, post 2008, believe. Buying a stock, bond, or mutual fund, then sitting on it while it fluctuates up and down is at best an era gone by. The reason is simple. Economic trends move so fast in today's culture what could be a good bet today could have a change in direction after the day's news cycle. Information travels at the speed of the internet and a tactical approach to investing would seem to be more appropriate, unless you are Warren Buffet and losing millions wouldn't affect your current strategy.

The simple reason "buy & hold" is better named "buy & hope" is because it lacks the ability to respond to markets in a timely manner. I will be covering much of this in chapter 8, but tactical management, in my opinion, is a more up-to-date management style for conservative investors. The average broker or investment advisor does the best he can by picking stocks, bonds and mutual funds that fit a client's risk tolerance.

Then for the most part, they sit on those assets come hell or high water, only liquidating in extreme situations. The reasons they change assets are to try to find "relative strength" in a sector or under-priced assets in a growing segment of the economy. Some use outside sources to get counsel on where they should invest next. These sources are investment advisors themselves trying to figure out the market. Usually what happens is the advisor picks a hot mutual fund manager and hopes he continues his track record. The whole system seems to look at returns over 1 year, 3 years, and 5 years to see who has the best record, or which fund or stock is "on the rise."

The problem with this mentality is it doesn't have a solid plan for how to manage risk. The markets do two things very well: they go up and they go down. Volatility is inherent in the markets. How you deal with volatility and risk should be the focus, not trying to compare returns. Comparing returns is tempting and you can make a case that certain fund managers have done well over time. Yet, everybody lost in 2008. When fear and panic set in, a buy and hold strategy will kill a retiree's portfolio. A fund manager has to pick stocks and in an environment like 2008 where the normal logic went out of the market, the fund manager was lost. He certainly couldn't sell everything, that's just not how they do it. And so they sat and painfully watched as their mutual funds value plummeted.

I'm sorry, but you have to do better than that if you are managing money for a conservative investor.

While there is no perfect system, a tactical approach doesn't make decisions based on returns; rather it looks at price movements in the markets along with other trend data to make portfolio adjustments. (You can read more about this in Appendix Four with articles written by Dan Hunt and Bryce Kommerstad.) Suffice it to say, that "buy & hold" is an antiquated model at best.

Buy and Hold is an effective conservative strategy, Maxim or Myth? You decide.

Wall Street saying #5: "Just buy a no-load index fund."

I have heard it said if you just bought index funds rather than mutual funds whose goal is to out-perform the S&P 500 index, you would have done better over the last ten years. There is probably some truth to that, depending on which "manager of the year" your advisor selected for you. The theory is the S&P 500 index fund from whatever company you choose will simply follow the index and beat the fund managers.

Let's say you were a conservative-minded investor in 2000 that didn't buy into the tech-bubble and invested heavily in the S&P 500 Index. You listened to John Bogle, founder of Vanguard, and purchased no-load, low expense index funds from several sources, investing $500,000. You were 55 years old and looking to retire in January 1, 2010, at age 65. Here is what happened to you.

S&P 500 from 2000-2009(6)

	S&P 500	**Your Account**
January 3, 2000	1455.22	$500,000
December 31, 2009	1115.10	$383,150
	-23.37% Loss	

Obviously, this is an over simplified illustration and you probably didn't have all of your money invested in the index funds. However, if you listened to the advice of those who believed this was a conservative strategy, you would have been incredibly disappointed with the funds you allotted to this strategy. Even if one third of your retirement accounts were in fixed assets that averaged 3%, over the decade you still would have lost about 8%. The important question is, would you want to retire with those losses or have to continue working?

Some say a decade like that will never happen again. Really? Are you willing to gamble your retirement on it not happening again? Is this truly a conservative strategy? I don't care if it's a no-load, low expense, Vanguard, Fidelity, ING, or any other group of index funds. If you just get the index with no way to secure your previous year's gains, your future is incredibly insecure.

Just buy an Index Fund, Maxim or Myth? You decide.

Wall Street Saying #6: "Index Annuities are Dangerous."

I love this one! Where do I begin? If you listen to a certain segment of the brokerage community, you would think index annuities are like great white sharks—they will jump out of the water and eat you whole!

It seems that there is a war going on between Wall Street and the Insurance industry. It's all about money, as usual. Every year between twenty to thirty billion dollars leaves the securities industry for these products. So, it is no surprise the securities industry who wants to stop the loss of commissions and fees from leaving their brokers have created an onslaught of negative publicity regarding index annuities.

There are tons of articles railing on Fixed Index Annuities (FIA), by supposed experts quoting their own research. Yet none of them compare with the most recent study completed in 2008 by David F. Babbel, Professor of Insurance and Finance, at the University of Pennsylvania's, Wharton School of Business.

Tom Cochrane interviewed Professor Babbel for AnnuityDigest.com. He is quoted in Mr. Cochrane's blog, July 2009:

> *"There has been a lot of misinformation in the popular press regarding FIAs. The vast majority of newspaper and magazine accounts vilify FIAs based on the results of alleged academic studies. The in-depth studies we conducted took over two years to complete and involved six Ph.D. financial economists and a pair of very well known senior actuaries....Our findings regarding actual products show that since their inception in 1995 they have performed quite well – in fact, some have performed better than many alternative investment classes (corporate and*

government bonds, equity funds, money markets) in any combination." (7)

Did you hear that? This professor from the well-known Wharton school of business does the definitive study to date on FIAs and the findings are very revealing, and very positive. These studies are done by academicians who, by their own admission, "don't have a dog in the fight." They are truly unbiased studies done for peer review and educational purposes.

Professor Babbel's study actually shows when FIAs are compared to alternatives like Vanguard's S&P 500 Index Fund, money markets, and the S&P 500 itself, gave better returns since 1995, and for each year they were issued. He makes the case that for those investors who have a conservative to moderate risk tolerance, FIAs provide what these investors desire.

Contrary to what some critics have stated, Babbel asserts that "Moderately risk-averse individuals will always choose the annuity over alternative investments." While the critics of FIAs have questioned whether people who could invest in alternative investments such as Treasury securities and equity mutual funds would not rationally invest in FIAs. Babbel concludes that many rational investors would actually prefer annuities over alternative investments. (8)

I'll have much more to say about FIAs in Chapter 7, but for now let's just agree that though there has been unwarranted negative press about the actual products themselves, it's obvious they are not the great evil as some misinformed brokers portray them. In fact, they are a positive option for the conservative investor.

Index annuities are dangerous, Maxim or Myth? You decide.

While I have been critical of a broken Wall Street culture, I don't want you to believe that all brokers are an altogether worthless group. In fact, the independent brokers who are out of the large wire house system are a hard-working crew with the best of intentions and, more often than not, excellent abilities. They are often well-trained and well-educated professionals. It's the myths that the culture perpetuates and the bias it comes from that need to change.

Well, are you at least questioning some of the wisdom of Wall Street? Or are you still in the back seat on Christmas Eve wondering if Santa's coming?

- Four -

Jump in…the Water's Fine!

Flathead Lake

I was born in Kennewick, Washington, and when I was about one year old, my family moved to Missoula, Montana, so I thought I'd go with them. Missoula was a great place to grow up. Since my grandfather was a Methodist minister, our family would spend a lot of time up north in the Methodist campground at Flathead Lake. I know the name sounds funny, but Flathead is the proud name of the Indian tribe and reservation in the area. Flathead Lake was beautifully nestled in the middle of the rugged Montana Rockies and had its own "Loch Ness Monster" myths. It was practically a playground for any kid with a vivid imagination.

My two older brothers and I would head out early for a swim, leaving our parents asleep in the rustic cabins. We would run to the end of the dock and leap into the water. Well, at least my brothers would take the plunge. Call me a conservative Conrad, but I would stop for a few moments and look into the water and wonder how deep it was, where the monster was, and especially how cold it was. My brother's would be yelling at me with teeth chattering, "C-C-Come on…j-j-jump in…the w-water's f-fine!" I don't know why, but each time I believed them. They are my brothers, right? Of course, they were lying just to see the expression on my face when I came up out of the water with my lips blue from freezing! The lake is just south of Glacier National Park, which is aptly named. The water is anything but *fine!*

A new model of investing? Really? Feel like jumping in?

Whenever someone starts to talk about change, people get just a little nervous, kind of like leaping into an ice-cold lake. They are especially anxious when it involves their finances. As I bring up the subject of a "new model of investing," people are stopped cold at the end of the dock, not wanting to jump in. The status quo looks so good because it's the "known vs. the unknown," the warm and worn, yet rickety dock versus the potentially cold waters of a new investment model.

The Status Quo Bias

Financial researchers tell us it's the "status quo bias" keeping us from jumping into a new model, even though the new model may be a better one:

> *"Most real decisions, unlike those of economics texts, have a status quo alternative—that is, doing nothing or maintaining one's current or previous decision. A series of decision-making experiments shows that individuals disproportionately stick with the status quo. Data on the selections of health plans and retirement programs...reveal that the status quo bias is substantial in important real decisions." (1)*

When faced with a decision between the dock and the water, we tend to stay on the dock, rather than risk plunging into a new environment. I get it. You're afraid of investigating the benefits of a new model just because it's not what you are used to. You are afraid it may be the financial equivalent to the Loch Ness Monster swallowing up your assets. Yet, I need to point out that if you stay on the dock you are currently on, you may very well end up back at the same point you are now, frustrated and fearful—aggravated with your investing results and afraid of what the future holds. Sounds like a monster to me.

Wall Street is Disconnected from Main Street

The main problem with Wall Street is that it is disconnected from Main Street. Wall Street just doesn't get it. My trainer John gets it. I am trying to get back in shape, or at least some resemblance of "in shape." So I wake up at 6:00am on Tuesday and Thursday and let John have his way with me. It's a love-hate relationship. I love what the results are and hate what I have to do to get there.

John is a highly-educated young man with a Masters degree in exercise physiology. He knows why and how an exercise will achieve a certain result. He demonstrates how to do the movement correctly. He then has me perform the exercise, pointing out how I'm doing it incorrectly. He tells me how the physics work in the movement of my arm and how the distance the muscle is from the joint makes certain movements harder others. He explains it in a way that I understand. It is important to understand the connection between muscle movement and joints when the third set rolls around and I am sweating profusely, wanting to take short cuts. I know why I have to do the exercise and what it will accomplish. Knowing the connection between doing the exercise correctly and achieving the results I desire keeps me going through tough times. And there are plenty of tough times.

When I told John I was a financial planner and I was writing a book on conservative investing, he made some interesting comments. John said that what he hears from Wall Street has nothing to do with the realities of his finances. He believes Wall Street is disconnected with reality. He told me what he hears on the financial networks from so-called experts just doesn't make sense when he thinks of his own investing. You know, I hear this from a lot folks.

Like John, the conservative investor is confused by Wall Street. Huge dollars, mega-deals, hot cars, expensive suits, fancy jewelry, and greedy advisors who each week it seems pull off investment scams bilking average investors out of their retirement savings. It seems like there is just no conscience.

The government regulators seem inadequate and unable to stop the onslaught of Wall Street greed.

What is the typical Wall Street model of investing? To begin with, it is based on a "greed is good" philosophy. Once you understand who it's "good" for, you will know why people get so discouraged.

How does the disconnected "greed is good" philosophy play itself out for the average American? Typically, Ma & Pa Lunchbucket are conservative investors who would like a plan designed specifically around their risk tolerance. What they actually receive is a diversified portfolio of market assets and asset classes managed in a "buy and hold" strategy with little movement over the years. Ma & Pa's "unique" portfolio consists of a basket of proprietary mutual funds, a variable annuity and possibly some blue chip stock, maybe even a bond or two. The mutual funds will be C-shares, which allow the broker to make a 1% trailer commission on Ma & Pa's assets with no motivation to change them over the years. They may receive one or two B-share funds, which carry penalties if you sell out of them too early, so you will be discouraged from leaving his services. This model is not only obsolete, but just plain wrong on many levels.

The second problem with Wall Street is it is too complicated. Wall Street forces you to rely on the professional to not just acquire the investments needed, but to decide *for* you what conservative looks like in a plan. The professional broker is swimming in the water saying, "Jump in!" Understandably, most conservative investors do not have a clue when it comes to evaluating and choosing stocks, bonds, mutual funds, annuities, or even know what a REIT is. They don't even know the majority of money markets are not FDIC insured! They are standing at the edge of the investing dock, anxiously wondering if this chattering teethed broker in the water knows what he's talking about with no way of being sure.

The average investor has spent an entire lifetime working hard at raising families and plugging away dawn to dusk in a non-investment related career. They have good reason to not have amassed the information and skill set needed to keep up with current investment strategies, the ever changing market conditions, and how they influence assets. Not only are they clueless on how to evaluate and choose an asset, they don't know how much of their money to put into an asset class and why. In fact they probably ask, "What the heck is an asset class anyway?" They listen to the TV and Radio "talking heads" for their information, not realizing that the majority of guest analysts are money managers looking for exposure in the media to promote their business. Tell me, what would you think a professional who manages a "large-cap, growth fund" would say about investing? Would he not be saying, "...come on in, the water's fine" even if it's glacier cold?

Financial commentators in the media are looked upon as the investment guru for millions. It's not that these media moguls are bad people or that they even give poor advice. They simply do not know who you are or your specific needs. They also assume you, the average conservative investor, know what the heck they're talking about when they recommend "no-load, sector funds..."or any other asset. Even if you did figure out what they were talking about, they didn't tell you where it fit in your portfolio of assets.

Remember, a media personality's number one job is to sell "air-time" and their next book. Their job description does not include finding out your specific situation and emotional response to market losses, make a plan that fits your needs and then review that plan on a regular basis. Uh-uh, not even close. With friendly tones and impressive sounding words, they sell you a simple solution in 90-second sound bites with commercials for their latest book or next broadcast. Not a good place to find personalized investment advice. Maybe it's okay for general information, but you need a lot more than generalized information.

Ma & Pa Lunchbucket & the Wall Street Model

Consequently, people realize they still need help and turn to some well-advertised, recognizable, name-brand, Wall Street brokerage house. Here's what the average experience is for Ma & Pa Lunchbucket trying to follow the Wall Street Model of Investing. They go to a seminar sponsored by a major brokerage firm's local office, conducted by a professional who is probably getting money for the cost of the workshop from some investment company who wants to promote their products. They sign a "complimentary consultation" form and head in for a visit with a supposedly "unbiased, trusted" advisor.

Mr. & Mrs. LB enter the offices and are shown the conference room. The broker is impressively dressed and surrounded by the aura of a Wall Street firm. Ma & Pa unveil their assets to the broker's waiting hand who says, "Not to worry…we'll take good care of you." The two conservative investors take a "risk-tolerance" exam to determine their feelings about gains and losses in a portfolio. They talk about goals and time lines, kids and grandkids, realities and dreams. Mr. LB tells of the last broker they were with and how they got burned and how they want safety with as little risk as possible. The broker acknowledges their concerns, telling them about the history of the prestigious firm for which he works. Mrs. LB is nodding approvingly. The broker invites them back in a week to hear the details of his specialized plan made specifically for Mr. & Mrs. LB. They leave with hope that the water may indeed be fine, this time.

Mr. & Mrs. LB come back for a plan they believe is designed just for them. Instead, they receive a cookie cutter group of investments the broker has been trained to sell. After viewing so many client statements from wire houses, I can actually predict what assets will be on the statement based on the company doing the investing. It is common knowledge among industry professionals that each major firm has a very predictable recommendation for each client. It may vary only by degree, but brokers are encouraged to make sales of the companies who own proprietary mutual funds and other assets that profit the investment firm over other, better, and more appropriate assets.

This is the Wall Street model and has been for years. Give Ma & Pa a belief that the plan is tailored to their specific needs, when in reality it's a group of assets the average conservative investor would never choose. They would gag if they understood the actual risk involved in the portfolio. Ma & Pa never really get what their conservative desires are after—a low risk portfolio. Yet, this is the Wall Street way.

In the long run, the average conservative investor needs a way to easily and confidently determine how and where to place their retirement assets. It's more than painfully obvious we need a new model, one Ma and Pa LunchBucket can understand with confidence. They might still need the assistance of a professional to execute the plan, but it would be Ma & Pa LunchBucket's plan, designed by Ma & Pa.

The final reason Ma & Pa LunchBucket need a new model is that Wall Street wire houses themselves don't believe in their own system.

> *"After a decade of pushing fee-based services, Wall Street is slashing and burning the infrastructure that has supported the business. The moves threaten to damage the long-term health of the wirehouse business model for financial advisers and their clients.*
>
> *On the new Wall Street, wire houses are gutting the home office staff that has driven the growth of fee-based business...Even getting a simple phone call returned from the home office is turning into a trial. Forget about one-on-one attention." (2)*

Remember, Wall Street has long run on the motto, "greed is good." This philosophy places those who sell the assets at the top of the food chain and the clients who buy the assets just plain camel fodder. So, if you feel like Wall Street's disconnected voice is calling to you saying, "come on in, the water's fine," get off the dock as soon as possible!

There is definitely a better way. There is a model out there that resonates with your conservative nature. It is proficient at connecting your desires with an appropriate financial plan, yet simple enough for every conservative investor to understand. It is the "ABC Model of Investing." Let me explain…before you jump in.

- Five –

Lego's, Train Sets, and the ABC Model of Investing

Easy? Really?

Do you get the same feeling I get when somebody tells you, "This is going to be easy"? I start to think back to the boxes at Christmas that read, "Some assembly required." Right! I spent hours trying to put together LEGO's, train sets, race car tracks, and tricycles. Okay, I'm not the most mechanically gifted Boomer out there. I got it. But, "easy?" Really?

I'm not sure Wall Street would like you to believe investing is easy, yet when I listen to the media talking heads on finances, my mind reverts to "some assembly required." (After all, if it was easy, you wouldn't need them, right?)

Wall Street's Pyramids and Risk Tolerance

Wall Street's typical model of investing starts with the "Pyramid of Assets" and moves on to "Asset Allocation" models, which seem anything but easy or simple to understand. As I mentioned in the first chapter, these models depend on the broker knowing your "risk tolerance," which is the degree of uneasiness an investor is willing to experience when there is volatility in their portfolio. In other words, if your portfolio is experiencing a downward movement and you tend to freak out quickly, you would have a lower risk tolerance. If you feel okay when your portfolio is down, believing it will rise with the tide, you have a higher risk tolerance. Again, a broker usually gives you a test to determine the degree of your risk aversion.

However, I'm fairly certain most conservative investors know they're conservative. Some might, in the back of their minds, consider themselves a moderate. I've never run into a conservative investor who, after telling me they were indeed conservative, turned out to be an aggressive investor. There's something about losing money that rankles the skin of a conservative investor. Fluctuations in the market just plain keep them awake at night! No kidding, they really lose sleep over it.

A Conservative Investor's Dilemma

Take Silvio and Lenora for instance. They are one of my all-time favorite client-partners. Lenora has told me more than once how she can't get to sleep at night. She's a worrier and a night owl. She doesn't think she would be able to sleep at all if they had money in the market. They don't want any market risk whatsoever. They understand the market goes up and it goes down and want to know only two things about their investments.

First, is their money safe from market losses, and second, are they beating CD's? They want that "in between space" of bank-type savings and market risk assets.

Silvio and Lenora are the type of investors who loves the ABC Model of Investing. They intuitively want the majority of their assets not open to market losses. Unlike Silvio and Lenora, some conservative investors will have a small to moderate percentage of their assets in the market. The problem is there are not many choices for this type of an investor. They struggle for years with low interest rates and long for the good old days of 12-15% CD's!

So, I have a few questions: How do you, the conservative investor, know where to allocate your money to avoid the volatility that gives you sleepless nights? How do you know which assets to use and why you might use them? How does an individual asset fit into the total picture? Can an average investor really understand why his or her money is placed in one investment over another? Do you need a degree in finance to understand it? Is there a simple way to understand how to allocate your assets to accomplish your goals? Could it be the broker needs to take your test, rather than you the conservative investor, needing to take their test?

The ABC Model of Investing

Let's take a look at the ABC Model of Investing and see how it helps the conservative investor easily understand how to allocate assets. Maybe then, you will have the answers at your fingertips.

First, imagine all your investible assets are liquid and we could arrange them in any way you like. That includes all your CD's, money markets, annuities, stocks, bonds, mutual funds, REITs, or whatever. It would be everything except your real estate, all liquid with no strings attached. Next, let's make a plan starting today.

You will have to imagine your assets not where they are invested today, or last year, or even where they were 10 years ago. We're not looking in the rear-view mirror, but trying to map out our future. This is vitally important, because you want to have your investments set up for your needs going forward, not left in accounts that might jeopardize your future. Of course, I realize not all of your assets are actually liquid and in a position to move to your ideal situation. This exercise will give you a glimpse of what you value in the types of assets in which you might invest and how to allocate them.

Category A: Cash

Let's divide assets into categories, A, B, and C, which represent three types of assets. Category A is your cash reserves. Cash assets potentially carry low returns, but the principal is guaranteed and interest is compounded. According to the Federal Reserve, the average 6-month CD rate from 1990-2009 was 4.37% (20 years); 2000-2009 was 3.32% (10 years); from 2005-2009 it was 3.99% (5 years).(1) It is interesting to note the average inflation rate from 2000-2009 was 2.57%, which leaves the five year return averaging less than 1.5% before taxes. (2)

These accounts are typically taxable and have optimum liquidity. However, they can also be set up in various tax advantaged strategies such traditional IRA's, Roth IRA's, etc. Most often, these are bank-held assets like CD's, savings accounts, and money markets.

Financial advisors will often refer to this as short-term money, or emergency funds. If your furnace breaks down, your roof leaks, or you have a medical emergency, category A is where you save for such an occurrence. If you are saving for an exciting vacation or a new car, this is where the money goes. It is also where you might want to keep a savings account to replace any income lost due to a prolonged illness, injury, or job loss. Commonly, financial advisors will tell you to have six months to a year of income put away for these instances. The illustration below shows Column A assets. Imagine them as "Yellow Money" accounts.

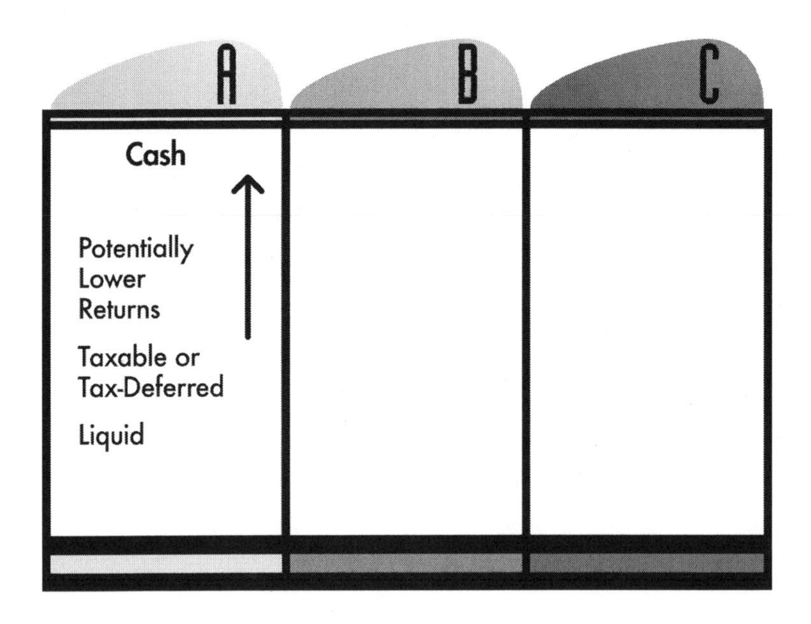

Category B: Fixed Principal Assets

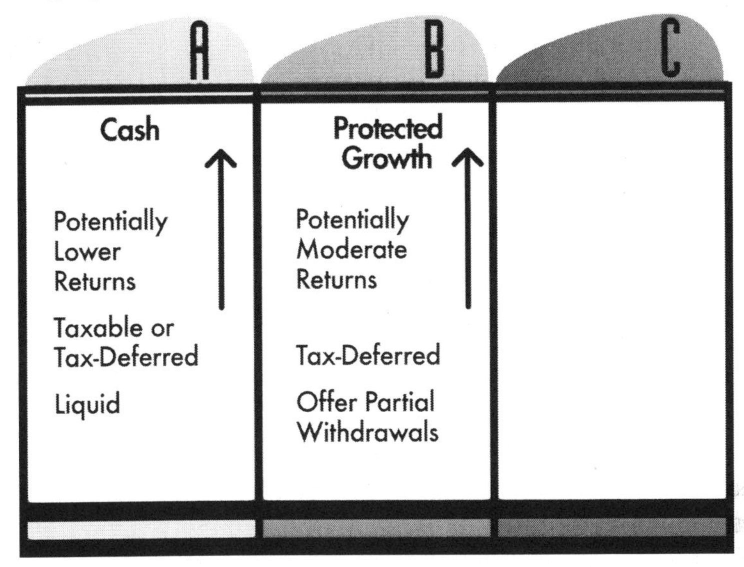

The second category is Column B, the "Green Money" column, and holds Protected Growth assets. They offer potentially moderate returns, are tax-deferred and offer partial withdrawals. The principal is protected, and previous years' gains are retained as interest. The annual returns on these assets vary greatly. In my own practice I have seen them yield from 0% to as high as 16%. Some include bonuses from 3% to 8%. These assets are designed to be the middle ground between CD's and the market. During the five-year period from October of 2004 through September of 2008, Index annuities averaged 5.42%, while CD's averaged 2.78%. (3)

I prefer using fixed indexed annuities in column B, which link the interest credits to the performance of a market index, such as the S&P 500, S&P Midcap 400, DOW, Russell 2000, Euro Dow, etc. Column B money is set aside for a longer period, often 5-10 years. Annuities have strings attached for withdrawals, but can be an excellent source of income over a lifetime. In other words, don't allocate money to the B column in which you would need more than 10% next year, especially considering there could be a tax penalty on certain withdrawals prior to age 59 ½.

Generally assets in this column offer only partial withdrawals without a penalty, yet many include riders that waive surrender fees in the event of a nursing home stay or terminal illness. Indexed annuities are designed to function as the middle ground between lower interest rates of bank and savings accounts, and potential higher returns of risk oriented market money.

This is the Fixed Principal Asset column, where the principal is protected. The ABC Model looks at Fixed Income Assets different than Wall Street does. Over the years, Wall Street has used a laddered portfolio of bonds to accomplish the goals of column B, yet a bond can lose value. From 1999 to 2009, if you were holding Lehman Brothers, Bear Stearns, ENRON, or World Com bonds, you might have thought you were safe, but found out just how much you could lose in a bond. If you are holding a California bond right now you might be a little insecure. That is why we use Fixed Principal Assets in column B rather than Fixed Income Assets.

In contrast to bonds, Column B has three Green Money Rules: protect your principal, retain your gains, and guarantee your income. If an asset can't do those three things, it doesn't belong in the ABC Model's Column B. Bonds don't follow those rules so they must go in the next column, column C. Therefore, a Fixed Indexed Annuity is probably an ideal asset for column B.

Currently, there are some indexed annuities with shorter surrender periods, enabling the conservative investor to ladder maturities to increase the liquidity over a 3 to 10 year period. We'll discuss this in detail in chapter seven.

Fixed Index Annuities (FIA) are becoming more popular among conservative-minded investors. Indexed annuities carry the guarantees of large insurance companies with billions of dollars of assets. FIA's number one characteristic is the number one characteristic conservative investors' desire: protection of principal! It is also the number one characteristic conservative investors believe a "fixed income asset" should have, but unfortunately doesn't. That's the GREEN column.

Category C: Risk

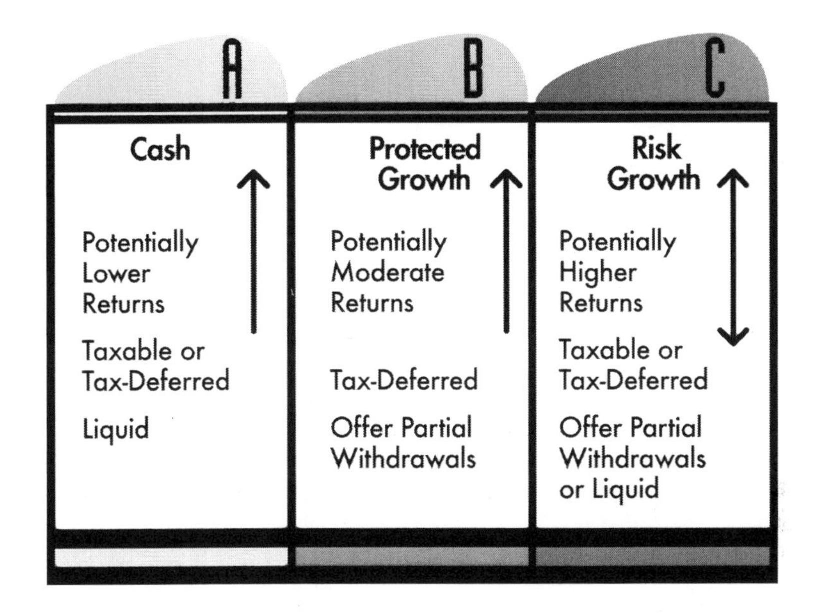

Column C represents our Risk Growth assets, which move up or down with the market. Investors usually chase higher returns over time, though these assets can gain or lose 30% in a year, or even more. The S&P 500 lost 38% in 2008, but the average of 1995-1999 was over 25%. (4) The market "giveth" and the market "taketh" away, there are no protections or limits. This money is invested in securities like stocks, bonds, mutual funds, variable annuities, options, REITs, and the like. The principal isn't protected and last year's gain may be lost in a downturn of the market. While these accounts are associated with a longer time horizon they are usually more liquid due to the "sellable" nature of securities, unless they are in a variable annuity which only offer partial withdrawals.

The majority of the assets found in column C are in retirement accounts such as 401(k)'s, 403(b)'s, IRA's, and variable annuities. Column C monies can also be found in the form of non-qualified (after-tax) brokerage accounts, mutual funds, stocks, or bonds, held by an individual, jointly, or even in trust. You can be your own manager or hire a professional investment adviser to manage this part for you. Let's paint these investments Red for Risk.

ABC Example

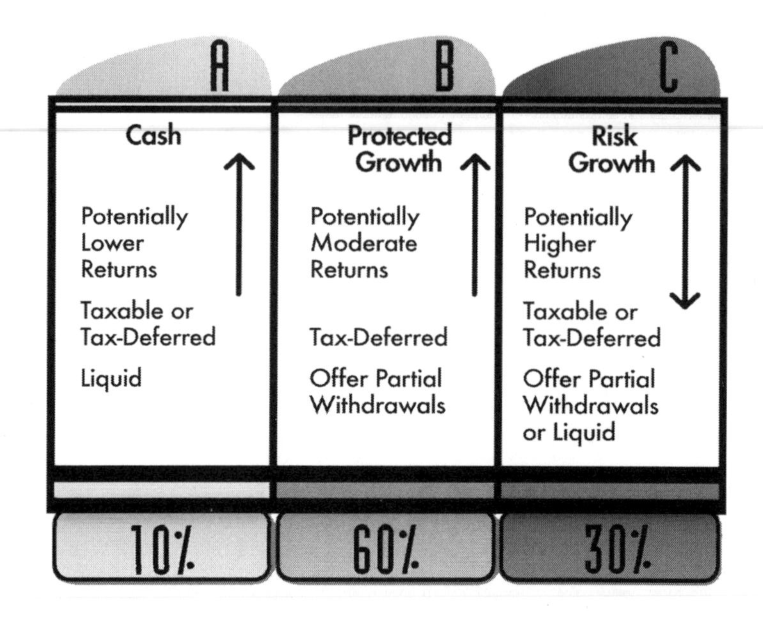

I think it would be helpful to see an example. If you had $500,000 of investable assets and wanted the 10/60/30 split illustrated above, you would have about $50,000 liquid in bank accounts (Column A), $300,000 in Fixed Index Annuities (Column B), and about $150,000 in securities such as stock mutual funds, bond mutual funds, or managed accounts. When we get to chapter nine, we'll discuss the power of this allocation versus a more growth-oriented portfolio. Needless to say, if the market experienced another 38% drop like in 2008, only 30% of your portfolio would be exposed to a loss. Seventy-percent would not have lost one red penny!

Create Your Own ABC Model

Now it's time to figure out how you would allocate your assets in the ABC Model. All you will need to do is ask yourself, "What percent of my total assets do I want in each column?" We will determine in the following chapters what specific assets to use, but for now try to use percentages in each column that "feels right" to you. There is no right or wrong answers. It is up to you, the investor, to look at the guidelines for each column and decide.

So, what percent of your investable assets would you like in each column? Go ahead and take a shot at it.

Start with column (A) and ask yourself how much emergency money or liquidity you need. In other words, don't worry much about returns, but concentrate on liquidity. How much money do you need available immediately? How much money would you need in the next six months to live on if your current income went away? You can express it in a percentage or a specific dollar amount. Your number will be personal to you.

Second, you could ask yourself how much money you want at risk in the market and what type of market risk you want. Do you want Stock-type risk or Bond-type risk? As a conservative investor you probably don't want options or aggressive risk oriented assets. Keep it simple here. Decide how much money you want at risk, and then decide what type of risk. The more conservative you are, the more you will gravitate toward bond-type risk. The more moderate you are, you'll probably have a higher percentage in this column and most of it will be in stock related assets such as mutual funds, ETF's, or managed accounts.

Again, just ask how much money you're willing to expose to losses. If you can't stand the thought of losing a penny, your answer to this question is zero! Go ahead and take a stab at it. Got your number? Let's move on.

Once you have the percentage you want in Columns A and C, simply add them together and subtract from 100 to get your B Column percent. It's that easy. You now have percentages in each column and can make adjustments. For instance, if you feel you have too much at risk simply put more in Columns A or B. Or if you feel you have too much tied up in Column B and don't want any more risk, then simply add more to Column A. Play with the numbers until you think you have what you want.

Types of Assets

Next, let's take a look at what type of assets are available in each column. As I said before, column A assets are bank assets such as CD's, money markets, savings accounts, etc. Column B assets are true Fixed Principal Assets. In other words, they are assets where your principal is protected from market fluctuations, and you retain previous years' gains. These would be assets like Fixed Annuities, Fixed Indexed Annuities, and Whole and Universal Life insurance cash values. Column C would contain assets such as stocks, bonds, mutual funds, variable annuities, ETF's, REIT's, hedge funds, Options, etc.

ABC Risk vs. Reward

Now let's take a glance at what you gain and lose in each column. There is a "Risk-Reward" for each column, which means you stand to gain or lose something by placing assets in each scenario.

If your main goal in placing money in column A is good liquidity, you will probably have to put up with low interest rates. So, you would be capturing *liquidity* and losing some potential *gains*. If you want the *protection* of Column B, then you will have to consider a longer-term mindset, putting up with 10% *liquidity* each year. If what you want by placing money in Column C is higher potential *gains*, you'll have to give up *protection* of those assets.

Said differently, in Column A you give up GAINS to get more LIQUIDITY. In column B you give up some LIQUIDITY to acquire PROTECTION from risk, and in Column C you give up POTECTION for higher potential GAINS, as illustrated below.

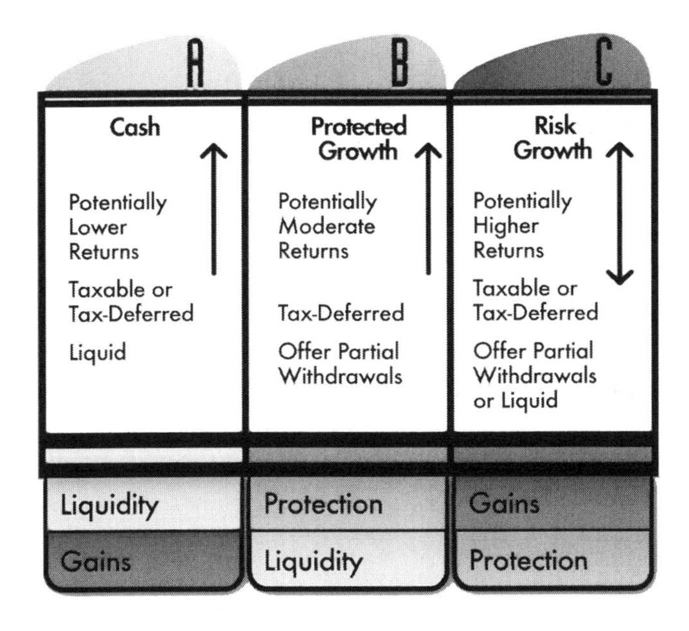

Rule of 100

Finally, like some of my clients, you might not have a clue how much money you want in each column and need a little guidance. It might be helpful to picture money as being either GREEN or RED—GREEN for Safe and RED for Risk. GREEN Safe money is money not exposed to risk in the market. RED Risk money is just that, money in the market.

It might also help to picture my friend Steve the Sleepless Investor. He's a 65-year-old retired salesman with $600,000 of investible assets. Steve's advisor suggests an often used formula called the Rule of 100 to help him determine how much he wants in Columns A, B, and C. Very simply he used the formula below of 100 minus his age, to determine how much money he wants in Green protected accounts and Red risk accounts.

RULE OF 100
100
-65 Investor's Age
35% Percent of Red Risk Assets

Steve decides to put 65% in the first two columns. Mr. Sleepless first determines he wants in 10% or $60,000 in Column A for an emergency fund, plus he's planning a "restful" vacation in Seattle. Next, he puts the balance of the green money portion from the Rule of 100 which is 55% or $330,000 in a laddered portfolio of indexed annuities in Column B. Steve has 35% or $210,000 left to be placed in Column C's Red Risk assets. He chooses a professional money manager who manages a conservative portfolio of funds.

Sleepless Steve's ABC Allocation of $600,000

Steve's Rule of	**100**	
Steve's Age	-65	
	35%	Percent of Red Risk Assets

Column A	Column B	Column C
10%	55%	35%
$60,000	$330,000	$210,000

Steve is finally able to find peace with his assets. Now he's on vacation, asleep in Seattle.

See how easy it is? Go ahead, give it a try. If Steve the Sleepless Investor can do it, you can too.

Major Differences Between Wall Street and the ABC's

The ABC Model of Investing simply asks you to determine your liquidity needs, and then how much you want at risk. Notice there are two major differences between the ABC Model and Wall Street. First, two out of three categories offer protection of principal. Bank assets are insured by the FDIC. Annuities are backed by the claims paying ability of large insurance carriers. Be sure and ask your agent or broker to inform you about the strength of the insurance companies they recommend. Second, the ABC's are easier for the average person to understand which gives the conservative investor confidence.

Protection and simplicity are keys in the ABC's. Yes, there is an allotment for Red Risk money, and the ABC Model makes it easy to determine how much risk a conservative desires. In the next three chapters, we'll discuss in detail each category's investments.

Now that you know how to divide your assets into categories for your Conservative Risk Tolerance, we'll take a more detailed look at what type of assets accomplish your goals in each of these columns. While it will take some time and consideration, it can't be as hard as the train set I put together on Christmas in 2000. Can it?

- Six –

Who's the King? Yellow Money Savings

Who is the King?

Do you ever notice how everybody wants to be King? I mean you have Burger King, King Tut, B.B. King, Martin Luther King, and Don King. How about the King of Carpets (cleaners), King of the Cage (martial arts), King of Pops (hand-crafted popsicles), King of Shaving (razor advertisers), King of Cars (A&E's TV show), and King of the Hill (kid's game). And who could argue that Elvis isn't the King of Rock-n-Roll?

There seems to be a lot of confusion, or at least a lot of puffed up ego's claiming their little portion of the world. Yet, when it comes to developing liquidity in a portfolio – Cash is King!

The Goal of Yellow Money

The goal of Column A, Yellow Money, is to provide a sufficient amount of liquidity for the majority of your portfolio while keeping it protected from losses due to fluctuations in the stock market. Remember, yellow money is money that typically earns lower returns, is guaranteed by FDIC, and can be liquidated with minimal expense and maximum efficiency. We are not expecting big gains in these assets because this is "cash." As a rule, the longer the time horizon for an investment, the greater the potential returns. When people say that money never sleeps, they're wrong. This money is fast asleep, earning very little, but is available and free from market risk.

Keep in mind Yellow money is short-term money. In other words, these are dollars you want to put away for short-term goals like planning for a vacation, buying a car, your grandson's tuition, a new furnace, a new roof, etc. Money should be thought of as having specific time frames associated with your goals. If the money is to be used in the next six months to two years, its short-term money. What you need is quick access with few strings attached in the form of penalties for early withdrawal.

You also want to have cash available in the event you can't work for six months to a year. You don't have to keep 6-12 month's salary available however you do want to have your basic living expenses covered. For example, if your monthly expenses total $2,500 and you wanted to cover six months, then you would need $15,000 in Yellow money accounts. If you wanted to cover a twelve-month budget at this rate you would need $30,000. In order to get the most interest, you could make use of CD's that mature after six to twelve months and ladder their maturities.

If you are planning to give cash as Christmas, Birthday, or Graduation gifts, you will want to time the maturity of these protected assets to coincide with the specific events. If your Grandson is graduating in 18 months, than a 12-18 month CD might give you the best rate of return with the principal guarantee you desire.

The reason you want to have Yellow money available for these short time-frame events is that you don't want to have to sell off long-term assets when they may be at a loss because of market fluctuations or early redemption penalties. Just imagine if you had to sell your mutual funds in the fall of 2008 to pay for a $5,000 furnace repair. If you had invested in a typical growth fund in October of 2007, which was a high point of the market, then sold a year later for the furnace repair, you would probably have sold into a nearly 40% loss. Not a good idea. If you play the asset game by the rules of each asset class, you will rarely have to liquidate an asset before its optimal time. That's why Column A investing is so important.

How much liquidity is necessary?

How much liquidity is right for you? That's a personal preference. You might be able to start with the six month expenses, then set aside for an emergency, and add to that any near term expenses on the horizon such as vacations, tuition, automobile purchases and repairs. It's often helpful to develop a budget in order to see these items more clearly. A sample budget worksheet is found in Appendix Two.

At any rate, you will want to determine either a dollar figure or a percentage of assets allotted for Column A giving you the liquidity and safety you desire. For instance, say you have $700,000 of investible assets. If you want $70,000 of Yellow money liquid, that would amount to 10% of your assets. Many of my clients tell me they like between 10% and 25% of liquidity in their portfolio in Column A. Remember, there is no right or wrong answers. Only you can determine what you need in Yellow money.

Two Yellow Money Categories

It's helpful to know Yellow money can be divided easily into two categories:

- Accessible with **no penalties** for early withdrawal
- Accessible with **minimal penalties** for early withdrawal

Let's take a look at positives and negatives of each asset in the two categories.

Accessible with no penalties for withdrawal

First on the list are checking accounts that banks and other savings institutions offer. While these are the most easily accessed funds, they are also the least profitable. They usually come with fees attached and no interest, though banks offer some interest-bearing accounts with the caveat of a high minimum balance. It's often wise to keep only your monthly cash needs in your checking accounts due to low interest.

Next you have FDIC Insured Money Markets that traditionally pay a higher amount of interest, yet still have checkbook access. It's important to note that not all money market accounts are FDIC insured and thus exposed to fluctuations in value, though usually minor. The risk is usually minimal because the people who manage the money market accounts invest in short term, even overnight securities. Still, it is better to have this money insured than open to risk.

Money market accounts come with various strings attached. One account might require an initial deposit of $10,000 while another account only requires $1,000. The larger the requirement, the higher the interest rate, though this may vary. Money markets have different options for customer withdrawals. Some have total checkbook access, while others limit the amount of checks used per month. Again, the less the access, the higher the interest rate usually is.

A common practice suggested by financial planners is to have all your general deposits, including pensions, social security, and automated deposits pour into your money market account. Then you can transfer enough money for your monthly bills out of the money market in to your checking account. Because the money market account usually receives higher interest, it assures your largest cash account receives the most amount of interest.

Finally, we have bank savings accounts generally paying somewhere between money market and checking account rates. These accounts do not usually have checking privileges and are being used less and less.

Accessible with minimal penalties for early withdrawal

First on the list of accessible assets that carry a minimal penalty for early withdrawal are Certificates of Deposit, or CDs as they are commonly referred to. CDs are the preferred yellow money savings vehicle of many retired Americans. The reasons are obvious. They can provide a modest rate of return while maturing at relatively short periods. The rates are determined by the banking institution and declared in advance.

Another attractive feature of CD's is the small penalties associated with early termination. Most CDs offer a penalty of half your interest, which is very minimal. If your three-month CD is paying 2% per year and you decide to pull out 6 weeks into the term, usually your penalty is only 1%.

CD rates have adjusted over the years with lows in 2009 under 1% APR to the early 1980's rates of 12%-18% APR.(1) As I illustrated in a previous chapter about my great grandfather's interest rate experience of the 1890's, you may have to wait a long time before rates are in the double digits again. However, "callable CDs" offer higher rates of return with minimal interest rate risk.

It's important to realize that CD interest is taxable each year. In other words, if you made 2% on your $100,000 last year, you would be adding the $2,000 you made to your income tax whether you take out the interest or not. That income may affect your tax bracket, social security taxation, and possibly your real estate tax, depending on the state you live in. It's kind of like "good news, bad news." You made $2,000 more, but it forced you into a higher tax bracket, made you pay taxes on 85% of your social security instead of 50%, and you lost the real estate tax exemption on your home. Come to think of it, was that lousy 2% rate worth all the trouble?

The last assets we look at in Column A are government savings bonds like EE and HH bonds. They really don't have a penalty for early withdrawal other than losing the full potential of the asset at maturity. Once you liquidate the bond you will have to pay taxes on the interest you received over the course of holding the bond. Savings bonds are different than CD's in that you don't pay taxes on the interest until you liquidate the bond. You could hold the bond 30 years and not pay interest until the end. The interest is included as income on your tax return in the year you liquidate. The good news is you made money, and the bad news is you owe Uncle Sam because you made money. While not very practical because they are cumbersome to liquidate, they are as safe an asset as you can get. These bonds typically offer lower interest rates.

A side not favorable to the saving bonds is once they mature—say at 30 years—the government stops paying interest. So, now you have to decide on when to cash them in. Most clients with large amounts in savings bonds liquidate over years so the interest doesn't put them into a higher tax bracket.

Savings, not Investing

Column A assets are generally not thought of as actually investing, but rather savings. In other words, the regulators look at cash accounts such as CD's, savings accounts, checking accounts, and FDIC-insured money markets, as savings vehicles not investments. That's because the only risk involved is interest rate risk, or the risk that you would have to hold a CD at 2% while others are being issued at 3%. While your principal is protected up to the FDIC limit, you are said to have "deposited" money in a savings instrument rather than "invested" money in a security. It's probably a good distinction to make, but it sometimes makes me wonder if regulators have way too much time on their hands!

Just a quick thought before we end this chapter. Some people believe they need all their money liquid all the time. Just think about that for a minute. If you had the $700,000 mentioned in the example above, would you really need all of it accessible at any moment? This is a common mistake amongst highly conservative investors. It is a method of investing that will lend itself to diminishing your buying power over time because of low rates not keeping up with inflation. Don't make this mistake. As you'll see in the next chapter, you can still have protection, but with potentially higher average returns.

As you can see assets allotted to Yellow Money, Column A is for liquidity and safety, pure and simple. Determine your liquidity needs and go from there. And remember, Cash is King, not Elvis!

- Seven -

"They are who we thought they were..." Green Money Premium

"They are who we thought they were..."

October 16, 2006, Monday Night Football produced one of the most mocked coaching quotes in NFL history. "The Bears are who we thought they were. They are who we thought they were..." (1) Famous words from Dennis Green, then coach of the Phoenix Cardinals after a horrible second half and fourth quarter meltdown. The Cardinals blew a 20-point lead in less than 20 minutes! Coors Beer even made one of their more hilarious commercials lampooning the press conference. "They are who we thought they were..." even became a favorite of ESPN announcers when trying to explain why any team couldn't take advantage of their opponent's weaknesses.

Living in Chicago and being an avid Bears fan, I was rolling on the floor laughing when Green pounded the podium saying, "...we let 'em off the hook!" He couldn't have been more right, (they did let them off a 20-point hook) and more wrong. As it turned out, the Bears weren't who Green thought they were as they went on to play in the Super Bowl in February while Green was fired in January 2007.

Fixed Income Asset or Fixed Principal Asset?

When it comes to designing a conservative portfolio, you don't want to be wrong and think you have something you really don't have, otherwise you will be at the podium crying "They are who we thought they were," and be as misguided as

Coach Green. This is especially true when it comes to assets where you believe the principal is guaranteed. If you are wrong, you might experience a complete collapse in your portfolio because the safe mix of assets you thought you had, you didn't have at all.

In the investing community, the term Fixed Income Asset can refer to a number of financial vehicles like Asset Backed Securities and even Derivatives. The most common Fixed Income Asset is a Bond. This illustrates how disconnected Wall Street is from Main Street. When Wall Street uses the term Fixed Income Asset, the average person believes their principal is guaranteed. In fact, a bond IS a fixed income asset because the phrase refers to the "income" being fixed. However, people don't hear "fixed income," they hear "fixed" and believe their principal is protected when in reality it isn't.

This may come as a surprise to some, but bonds can lose value. Just ask those who held ENRON bonds, WorldCom bonds, Lehman Brothers, or Bear Stearns bonds. If you are holding California bonds you might be just a little nervous, too. You are told that if you hold the bond till maturity you will get your money back. There are NO GUARANTEES!

Choosing the right assets for Column B is crucial to a balanced, conservative portfolio. Assets should have what you think they should have, if you choose the right ones. You should gain security through the one element most investors think of when they hear the word "fixed" as it relates to an asset, which is protection of your principal. So, let's use the term Fixed Principal Asset to describe the financial vehicles we will use in Column B.

It is helpful to use these three Green Money Rules when choosing assets for Column B.

Green Money Rule #1: Protect Your Principal

Any asset in this category must have protection of principal if you follow the asset's rules. In other words, if you stay to term you must be guaranteed your principal in return.

Green Money Rule #2: Retain Your Gains

Over the contract term any gains you receive in this asset class are secured, unless of course you decide to withdraw the dollars and spend them.

Green Money Rule #3: Guarantee Your Income

Assets in Column B must have the ability to guarantee income in some manner. Isn't that what you actually think you have in a Fixed Income Asset? Well, maybe not.

It's a common misconception amongst investors that Bonds would fit in Column B. They don't. The reason is simple. There are no bonds that obey all three Green Money Rules! They are not who we thought they were! Bonds belong in Column C.

There is an asset that obeys all three rules. It is a Fixed Indexed Annuity (FIA) or even just a Fixed Annuity. An Indexed Annuity is a contract with an insurance company for an income, funded by an initial premium, whose interest is linked in some manner to an index in the stock or bond market. Principal is guaranteed, gains are retained, and an income stream is guaranteed in the form of an annuity payment or guaranteed withdrawal benefits. Let's take a closer look at how it works and how it fits in Column B's Green Money strategy.

So, what is an Annuity?

Most people have heard negative reports in the media about annuities. True, there are some drawbacks in owning an index annuity, which we will discuss. Also, some annuities are worse than others as we'll see. Yet, you don't throw away a whole class of assets simply because of a few bad apples. Would you stop buying mutual funds because you lost 48% in the XYZ Mutual Fund in 2008? Would you stop investing in bonds because of the Enron debacle? Probably not. While you may be a little more gun shy, you would not rule out investing in mutual funds or stocks because of losses or scandals. You would look as silly as Dennis Green in a Coors commercial! Of course there are bad stocks, mutual funds, bonds, and other investments. Your job is to find the good ones.

An annuity, technically, is a contract with an insurance company for an income payment either now or in the future. The word annuity means "payment." It's all about the payments to you! If the payment is now, the annuity is called an "immediate annuity." If the income payment to you is in the future, then the annuity is called a "deferred annuity" because the payment is deferred. It can be a Single Premium Deferred Annuity (SPDA) or a Flexible Premium Deferred Annuity (FPDA). You can purchase the annuity with a single lump sum as in a SPDA or make premium payments in a FPDA. By the way, they call the deposits into an annuity "premiums" because you are purchasing a guaranteed payment. They don't call them deposits as in a Certificate of Deposit or an investment as in a stock or mutual fund.

Pretty simple, huh? Immediate payment or deferred payment. Single premium or flexible premium. From here there are two widely divergent camps of annuities: Fixed and Variable. Though these two types of annuities are different, one thing remains the same. They remain a contract with an insurance company for a payment. However, what happens to your premium is where the diversity occurs.

For our purposes in Column B Green Money strategies, we will only be talking about Deferred Annuities. Remember, this is an annuity where your payment from the insurance company is deferred until you choose to receive it. It is important to note here the vast majority of annuity contract holders never exercise the option for the payment. They either use it as a long term investment for the earning potential or simply pass the asset on to heirs, which by the way in most cases avoids probate.

Variable Annuities

The question is what happens to your money sitting at the insurance company? You are expecting some type of a return, right? Absolutely! This is where the fixed annuity differs greatly from the variable annuity. Put simply, the variable annuity puts the risk of the principal on the investor, while the fixed annuity puts the risk on the insurance company. Let me explain.

When you purchase a variable annuity, your premiums go into a fund at the insurance company. The company offers you the option to choose from a varied amount of side accounts which are much like mutual funds. In fact, though they are not technically mutual funds, they are managed by the same managers and are after the same results. You might have portfolio options like American Funds, T. Rowe Price, Janus, Fidelity, ING, etc. They would typically give you a range of fund strategies from Growth to Value, and Emerging Markets to Domestic, and even some Bond Funds. You will pay management fees inside these funds along with other fees and expenses typical of variable annuities. These expenses range from 1.25% to 5% depending on the amount options you choose for your variable annuity.

For instance, you will always have what's called a Mortality and Expense Fee (M&E) of around 1.15% to 1.5%. These fees pay for the death benefit and general expenses inside the annuity that an insurance company incurs. Add to that an enhanced death benefit that guarantees not only your deposit, but increases your benefit to heirs in some manner. The cost varies, but might be .75%. Then you might want to choose a popular guaranteed income option or withdrawal benefit. These options might cost an additional .75%. If you add up where we are so far it looks like this:

M&E Charges	1.25%
Enhanced Death Benefit	.75%
Income Benefit	.75%
Fund Management Fees	.65%
Total	3.4%

You can see how these expenses might add up rather quickly as they provide increasing benefits. Also, because it's a variable annuity, your account statements will fluctuate and you can lose principal. Your potential for a higher gain than a traditional fixed annuity is greater, yet your exposure is more significant.

While some financial planners question the validity of variable annuities, they will certainly fit in more risk tolerant types of investors, but it is definitely not a Column B Green Money Asset. It breaks Rule #1, Protect Your Principal. So, if you are going to use it, you should think of it as a Column C Red Money asset.

Fixed & Fixed Indexed Annuities

Cleary then, the main characteristic of a Fixed Annuity is the protection of your principal. How then does a fixed annuity gain in value? Unlike a Variable Annuity, a Fixed Annuity guarantees principal and credits interest to your account, normally on an annual basis. It's this interest crediting that separates traditional fixed annuities from fixed indexed annuities.

We have already established that the fixed annuity guarantees principal and is not exposed to market risk. The insurance company in a traditional fixed annuity announces the interest it will credit for the year in advance, much like a bank announces its interest rate on CD's. It is compounded and tax-deferred. The subtle contrast in an indexed annuity is how the company determines the amount of interest to credit. An indexed annuity's interest rate is tied to an index such as the S&P 500. If the index goes up, the owner of the annuity is credited with a portion of the increase in the index and those gains are retained in the contract. If the index goes down, both the principal and previous years gains are retained, and the owner of the annuity loses no ground.

For instance, if the owner of the FIA pays a premium of $100,000 and at the end of the first year the market index goes up, say 10%, the contract would receive a portion of that gain, say 5%. That gain would be credited as interest and not subject to market fluctuations in the next year. Interest gains are usually credited on anniversary dates. So, if you purchased the annuity on May 21st, then the date your interest would be credited the next year would be May 20th, and you would then start a new year.

What are the guarantees?

Fixed Indexed annuities are guaranteed by the issuing insurance company who provides a contractually stated guarantee in each annuity. Insurance companies offer a minimum guaranteed return by using a 1%-3% interest rate on a portion of the initial premium for the duration of the contract. This enables the contract holder to receive their premium back at the end of the surrender period. Usually, the insurance company uses something less than 100% of the principal upon which to credit the minimum interest. For example, an insurance company might credit a minimum of 2% on 87% of the premium, as seen below:

FIA Guarantee Example:

Premium:	$100,000
87% of Premium:	$87,000
Minimum Interest:	2%
Number of Contract Years:	10
Minimum Guaranteed Balance:	$106,053

Though the gain isn't much over ten years, it does guarantee principal plus some interest. In this way, indexed annuities differ greatly from their cousin variable annuities. The insurance company assumes the risk of the asset in the fixed indexed annuity, while the investor holds all the risk with a variable annuity.

It's also important to note that insurance companies are regulated by the State Insurance Departments of each state, not the Securities and Exchange Commission. Company's investments and business practices are under the very watchful eyes of the State Insurance Commissioners. If an insurance carrier is headed for trouble in its ability to pay its claim, the commissioner steps in and sends the carrier to rehabilitation. If the company isn't able to make it through rehab, it is sold off to other carriers who take on the obligation of the insolvent company. In this way, insurance companies and the individual states have done a superb job of overseeing the industry, and the safety of client assets.

Remember Green Money Rule #1, Protect Your Principal is the battle cry of the Fixed Indexed Annuity.

How does an FIA credit interest?

Indexed Annuities have a wide range of options the contract owner can select from to link the interest rate to the market. These options are called "crediting methods" and can usually be changed annually. The owner of the contract selects which crediting option or options they want to use each year, deciding what percent of the total account value to put into each crediting method. Somewhere around the anniversary date, the insurance company allows the owner to change the allotment of values in the crediting options. Insurance companies tend to be innovative in their crediting methods for Indexed Annuities by changing how they calculate the link to the market. The following is just a sample of crediting methods:

Fixed Rate – Indexed annuities usually carry an option of a one year fixed interest rate. They announce the rate each year and also have a minimum guaranteed rate this strategy can never go under.

S&P 500 Annual Point to Point with a Cap – In this method, the interest is tied to the S&P 500 for the contract year and is given a cap on how much interest can be credited. The "point" referred to is the anniversary date of the contract. So, between the first anniversary date (point #1) and twelve months later (point #2), the insurance company looks at how the S&P 500 performed.

For example, if the market moved 10% in a year with a 5% Cap you would receive a 5% interest credit. In other words you would get 100% of the upward movement in the market up to 5%. If the market goes up 5% you get 5%. If it goes up 20% you get 5%. It's important to note that caps can change and they usually come with contractual minimum guaranteed caps. For instance, the lowest cap the insurance company can use for the year might be 1.5%.

One of the most attractive features of this type of indexed crediting is the company will reset the point at where the annuity calculates the interest each year. So, if the S&P 500 Index was at 1000 on your first anniversary date, the company would use that number as the starting point to figure that year's interest. If the index finished the year below 1000, say 850, your annuity would "reset" the starting point to 850 and calculate from there for the following year. In that way you are only looking at individual anniversary years rather than trying to beat the annuity's first year starting point five years down the road. This function is called "annual reset" and works in the favor of the contract holder.

Imagine if you didn't have this feature in your indexed annuity, and had to rely on a ten-year window. If that had happened from 2000 to 2010 you would have had virtually no gain in your asset! So, annual reset or even bi-annual reset is an incredible feature.

S&P 500 Annual Point to Point with a Participation Rate – This option is a take on the first method, but instead of using a cap the company will issue a rate at which your contract can "participate" in the gain of the market. So, if you have a 50% participation rate and the market went up 10%, you would receive 5%, if it went up 20% you would receive 10%. Again the insurance company has a minimum guaranteed participation rate at which they can never go lower.

S&P 500 Monthly Point to Point with a Cap – Here is a variation of annual point to point with the insurance company looking at individual months to determine the gain in your contract rather than years. The company will issue a cap on each month at the beginning of the contract year. They will then look at each month individually, adding them up at the end of the year to determine the rate of return. It is important to know that the Cap is an "upside" cap. There is no downside cap. Let me illustrate. Assuming a monthly cap of 2% let's look at a 12-month cycle:

S&P Monthly Point to Point with Cap Example:

Contract Month	S&P500 Return	Annuity Percent
1	2%	2%
2	3%	2%
3	1%	1%
4	-3%	-3%
5	0%	0%
6	-1%	-1%
7	1%	1%
8	2%	2%
9	5%	2%
10	1%	1%
11	3%	2%
12	0%	0%
Total	14%	9%

Notice in the graph above that in months 2, 9, and 11 the market went up more than 2% and the annuity was only credited with the 2%. Actually, it wasn't credited during the year. The company waits to total the numbers until the end of the year and then credit the interest to the contract. In year 4 the market went down more than the 2% cap and the whole negative number was put into the equation. If this ever created a situation where at the end of the year the total was negative, the annuity would get 0%. This is good if the market actually had a down year and you didn't lose anything, yet it can also create a lower return in a year that has a significant volatility between the months that wipes out gains for the year. This method has the potential to credit much higher gains in a market trending upward, but can create zeros in volatile years. When the market has a down year, Zero is your Hero!

S&P 500 Monthly Average with a Cap or Participation Rate - As illustrated with the first two crediting methods, this method uses a cap and/or a participation rate. Yet, different from the monthly point to point, it averages the twelve months between anniversaries. If the market is really hot in the first three quarters yet suffers losses in the last quarter, this method saves the year. Very simply, the insurance company keeps a record of the percentages of the movement in the market on a monthly basis, then divides by 12, applies the cap or participation rate for the final result. This is historically the least effective method.

Multi-Year with a Mix of Interest and a Percentage of the Market – One of the great innovations in the indexed annuity business is the invention of a new multi-year strategy that combines a percentage of the market with an interest rate. This is one of the few index annuities that charge a fee, but the fee is different than the fees on a variable annuity. The difference is the variable annuity charges fees regardless of annual performance and is on the entire account value. This indexed annuity has fees only on the gain in the annuity. If there's no gain there's no fee. The back testing on these types of annuities has been very promising. They are popular because of their innovation and fewer moving parts.

While Multi-Year annuities don't make use of an "annual reset" feature, they usually offer a two to five year reset period. Purchasing two to five year options in the market are generally less expensive than shorter term options. Thus the insurance company has the ability to pass through more interest to the contract holder.

Other crediting methods include the use of additional indexes such as the Dow Jones Industrial Index, Russell 2000, S&P MidCap 400, EuroDow, Hang Seng (China) Index, US Treasury, Barclay's Aggregate Bond Index, as examples. Companies use one, two, and three year monthly point to point strategies, multi-year monthly averaging, high water mark, and vesting schedules as alternatives for crediting methods. An excellent resource for researching crediting methods is Jack Marrion's website www.IndexAnnuity.org. He lists various companies and their current rates.

Crediting methods are the tools that help Index Annuities lock in returns. Remember Green Money Rule #2, Retain Your Gains!

Any Fees in FIA's?

Generally, indexed annuities have no fees. That doesn't mean there isn't a cost associated with an indexed annuity. It simply means that the cost is accounted for internally within the insurance company in most cases. Some of the newer versions of multi-year crediting methods come with fees on the gains as mentioned above, but other than that the only fees associated with indexed annuities are related to added benefits such as income riders. There are no mortality and expense fees or enhanced death benefit fees in most index annuities.

It sounds just a little odd to say there are no fees in indexed annuities, but you would have to understand how these assets are structured at the insurance company to understand why there are generally no fees.

First, the money you put into an indexed annuity with an insurance company is generally invested in high grade bonds, mostly government bonds. These bonds pay an interest rate to the insurance company. Let's say the bond yields 6%. The insurance company takes a portion of the interest for its profit and expenses and then there is what's called "excess interest."

In an indexed annuity, the excess interest is invested in call options in the market index related to the annuity crediting method chosen. Call options are contracts that give the holder the right to buy a security at a specified time in the future. The call option is valuable if the security it's tied to goes up and worthless if it goes down in the contracted time frame. This process allows the insurance carrier to build in profit, pay for costs such as an agent, and provide an attractive benefit to the contract holder.

What about liquidity?

If the benefit of an indexed annuity is a potential for a higher gain than other fixed assets then the drawback is its long term nature. In order for the insurance company to create a win-win situation for themselves and the client, the money has to stay put for a while so the underlying investments have time to work the way they are designed. This is the reason that annuity companies have surrender penalties associated with early withdrawals. These surrender penalties usually decline on an annual basis, say over a 5 to 10 year period. There are annuities with longer surrender periods.

Remember, these penalties are for any monies liquidated in excess of the penalty free withdrawal options or for total early withdrawal. Early withdrawal means you might have had an annuity with ten years of declining surrender penalties and totally liquidated in the third year, thus creating a penalty. A ten-year declining surrender period might start with a ten percent penalty in the first year and decline one percent a year for ten years. In the eleventh year you could withdraw all the money in your annuity without any penalty.

I would classify an indexed annuity as "moderately liquid." The reason is most indexed annuities have the ability for the contract holder to withdraw 10% of the cash value on an annual basis through penalty free withdrawals. The companies also provide the availability for annuity payment options at certain points over the contract years. That means you can turn the asset into a guaranteed income stream that you can't outlive.

In comparison, other assets such as CD's offer a different form of liquidity. A certificate of deposit is liquid at the end of the term which is anywhere from 3 months to 5 years. A bond's principal is only liquid at the end of the bond term or if the holder sells, which could be at a loss. A stock or mutual fund is always liquid, but the same problem of selling at a loss remains. It wouldn't be good advice to have monies in a mutual fund or stock that you had to liquidate on a monthly or annual basis for income purposes. They are generally not looked on as income bearing assets, unless they are paying dividends.

Indexed annuities are not only moderately liquid, but most make provisions in the contract that allow for more than the ten percent penalty-free withdrawals in the event of long-term care needs, disability, or terminal illness. In most cases these provisions allow you to withdraw 100% of your money before the contract term is over without any penalties.

Laddered maturities of FIA's

One of the best methods to use in Green Money Strategies in Column B is to ladder the maturities of indexed annuities. By maturity, I am referring to the time in an annuity contract when there are no longer any surrender penalties for early withdrawal. As we stated above, indexed annuities are long term in nature and carry early withdrawal penalties. Laddering the surrender years can create liquidity in the portfolio over time.

For example, you might start with a five year surrender charge annuity, followed by a six year annuity, then seven, eight and so on. I would prefer not going over 10 years in surrender charges, but there are some planners who use 12 to 16 year surrender periods. Many states are adopting a 10-10 rule that requires annuities sold in their state to have no greater than 10 years with surrender penalties that start with a 10% penalty in the first year and decline to 0% over ten years.

To illustrate, let's assume you wanted to allocate $300,000 in Column B. You could have five annuities with $60,000 in each one, starting with an annuity that has five years of surrender penalties and ending with a ten year annuity. You could even get bonuses in some of the annuities. That's right, bonuses. Insurance companies will offer bonuses for monies that stay longer in the contract. For instance, you can get an 8% immediate bonus on your account in a ten year annuity. If you put the $60,000 in, the first day it becomes $64,800 and any interest for that year is compounded on top of that figure.

Here's an example of a laddered maturity of five index annuities using hypothetical insurance companies:

1. XYZ Insurance Company – **5 Years**
2. Integrity Insurance Company – **6 Years**
3. American Insurance Company – **7 Years**
4. Super Life & Annuity Company with a 3% Bonus – **8 Years**
5. Big Daddy Insurance Company with an 8% Bonus – **10 Years**

Some agents struggle to find out how much to put in each annuity. As I stated above, you could split a $300,000 account in equal $60,000 amounts. However, if you wanted to create greater liquidity at a faster rate you could use larger amounts in the shortest term annuities and smaller amounts with the longest annuities.

The following is a comparison for planning using a ladder vs. not using a ladder:

Panning without a Ladder

- Usually one long term annuity
- Lack of liquidity
- Crediting methods of only one company
- Safety related to only one company
- No diversity in performance or management
- Larger commissions for the agents

Planning with a Ladder

- Multiple shorter term annuities
- Liquidity develops over years
- Diverse crediting methods by various companies
- Safety of multiple companies
- Diversity in performance and management
- Smaller average commissions for agents

In the end, using laddered maturities of index annuities offers the conservative investor a high degree of security along with moderate liquidity.

Planning for Income with an Indexed Annuity

One of the greatest needs of retirees will be to plan for income in retirement of 30 years or more. More on this subject in Chapter 10, "The Cowboy Preacher," but for now we need to talk about the income guarantees associated with indexed annuities that are changing the retirement planning landscape.

Income guarantees are the latest phase of indexed annuity innovation. Companies seem to be coming out with new guaranteed income or withdrawal benefits every month. It is an exciting phase of industry ingenuity that should go on for years.

Basically, there are two ways to get money out of an annuity. You either "annuitize" or "withdraw." The major difference is what happens to the account value when you choose either of these two options. You could probably understand annuitization best if you think of it as a pension payment. When you retire from a company, sometimes you are offered a choice between a lump sum and a monthly payment. If you take the lump sum, you receive a one-time cash payment of your retirement benefits from that company, and typically you invest it to create the income you desire. Yet, if you opt for the pension payments your company will send you a monthly check for the rest of your life or for the rest of you and your spouse's lives in some manner.

Here's a question for you. What happens to the principal once you select the pension payments? That's right. It is no longer available to you. The company uses it to fund your payments. No more lump sum availability. That is exactly how annuitization works. You receive a payment and there is no more cash available in the form of a lump sum. Actually corporations that offer pensions use annuity companies to produce this benefit.

You can receive payments guaranteed in various manners from an annuity. A common falsehood propagated by an uneducated press is once you choose payments from an annuity company and die, say after just two payments, the company will keep the rest of your money. While this is one option in an annuity contract (called "life only"), it is certainly not the only option and is definitely the least used for obvious reasons. I always say that in an annuity contract there are features which benefit the company and features which benefit the client. You need to know which ones are good for you and choose those.

Annuitizing has some tremendous opportunities for you as you retire. You can choose a joint-life option for you and your wife, which creates a payment for the both of you until…well, you know... you expire. You can even choose to have a certain amount of years guaranteed in addition to payments for the rest of your life. For example, you may want to guarantee payments for the first 10 years to you or your heirs. If you lived past the ten years, you would receive payments for as long as you live. You could guarantee payments for not only the first 10 years, but 15, 20, or more years. This method is called "life with a ten-year certain" or "20-year certain and life." Keep in mind that the more you have the company guarantee, the smaller the payments. That's why "life only" payments get chosen because they are usually the highest dollar amount. Check out the options in your contract, or have your agent go over those options with you.

Annuitization is clearly a Green Money Rule #3 benefit! Guarantee Your Income!

Guaranteed Withdrawal Benefits

Next, and probably the cutting edge of annuity development are the "Guaranteed Income Benefits" or "Guaranteed Withdrawal Benefits." These offer the best of both worlds, the availability of your cash account to stay liquid and a guaranteed income stream. Here's how it works.

First, you need to understand that insurance companies have the ability to account for the money in your contract in various ways, at the same time. Here are a few examples of accounts in a typical indexed annuity:

- **Accumulation Value**

  The current value of your annuity's cash account which includes any bonus and all interest credits to date, less any withdrawals.
- **Income Account Value**

  The current value of your annuity's income account which includes any bonus and all interest credits to date, less any withdrawals. Note: there is no cash value here.
- **Current Surrender Value**

  The current value of your annuity's cash account which includes any bonus and all interest credits to date, less any withdrawals, and minus any surrender charges that would apply if you chose to liquidate.

- **Guaranteed Minimum Surrender Value**
  The current value of your annuity's cash account which includes any bonus and the *minimum guaranteed* interest credits to date, less any withdrawals, and minus any surrender charges that would apply if you chose to liquidate.

This is certainly not a complete listing of accounts that an insurance company can provide, all of which are listed on your annual statements. As you can see, an insurance company has the ability to use different accounts in the same annuity, with the very same money, at the same time. This allows them to offer optional benefits that other assets, like CD's or mutual funds, can't possibly match.

An insurance company utilizing a guaranteed withdrawal benefit (GWB) offers a rider, (an amendment to your contract), which you can choose to accept or reject. These riders come with fees so you surely want the option to choose. The rider has two elements. It comes with a guaranteed interest rate and a guaranteed withdrawal percentage. The interest rate is credited to your initial premium and bonus each year for a declared number of years. This interest rate will increase your "income account value" only, and not your "accumulation value." In other words, it is not for cash value growth, but rather calculates the account value from which you may withdraw a guaranteed amount.

The withdrawal percentage is also guaranteed in your rider. It may range from 3% to 7%, depending on your age. In other words, you are guaranteed a lifetime of withdrawals based on the percentage stated at the age you choose to start withdrawals. For instance, the guaranteed income account growth rate might be 6.5%, and if you were to withdraw funds starting at age 70 you would be able to withdraw 5% of the accrued value. Some companies now offer inflation protection on the withdrawals, increasing them by 3% per year or some other formula for the growth of the withdrawal. Typically the withdrawal percentages increase with age, as illustrated below, and are different for each company:

Guaranteed Withdrawal Percentage:

Ages 60 – 69 4-5%
Ages 70 – 79 5-6%
Ages 80 & up 6-7%

Let's combine the guaranteed growth rate and the guaranteed withdrawal percent to see how it works:

Guaranteed Withdrawal Benefit Example:

Guaranteed Income Account Growth Rate: 6.5%
Bonus: 8%
Premium: $100,000
Age at Issue: 60
Age Withdrawals Chosen: 70
Guaranteed Withdrawal Percent: 6%
Income Account Value: $202,731
Guaranteed Annual Withdrawal Benefit: $12,164

The $12,164 annual withdrawal is guaranteed for life, no matter what happens to the accumulation value, which by the way would continue to earn interest credits attached to the indexes chosen. In order to match this feat, you would have to find an asset that returned a shade over 7.7% every year for the rest of your life, assuming a 15% net tax rate! That's the incredible power of a guaranteed withdrawal benefit.

At any time you can stop the income and take the remaining cash, less any applicable surrender charges, which most likely wouldn't exist at this point in the illustration. Just think of it, a guaranteed income stream along with the ability to walk away with a lump sum. This clearly isn't your daddy's pension plan, and it definitely obeys Green Money Rule #3…Guarantee Your Income.

Column B Green Money Premium is Fixed Asset investing done best by using Fixed Income Annuities simply because, like no other asset, "…they are who we thought they were!"

Disclosure: Past performance is no guarantee future results. Crediting rates including caps for FIA's can change and are determined by the insurance companies at the time of issue. Future performance cannot be predicted or guaranteed. FIA's are not registered as a security with the SEC and is not invested directly in any stock, bond, or security investment. FIA products, features, and benefits vary by state.

Annuity Contracts are products of the insurance industry and are not guaranteed by any bank or insured by the FDIC. When purchasing a fixed indexed annuity, you own an annuity contract backed by the insurance company, you are not purchasing shares of stocks or indexes. Product features such as interest rates, caps, and participation rates may vary by product and state and may be subject to change. Surrender charges may apply for early withdrawals. Be sure to review the specific product disclosure for more details. Guarantees are based on the financial strength and claims paying ability of the insurance company.

This information is not intended to give tax, legal, or investment advice. Please seek advice from a qualified professional on these matters.

Lifetime income benefit riders are used to calculate lifetime payments only. The income account value is not available for cash surrender or in a death benefit. Excess withdrawals may reduce lifetime income and may incur surrender charges. Fees may apply. Guarantees based on the financial strength and claims paying ability of the insurance company. See specific product disclosure for more details.

- Eight -

How's the Weather?
Red Money Investing

A Day at Wrigley (Well, a couple of hours at least)

I remember a few years ago, a friend gave me four tickets to the Chicago Cubs game against the Cincinnati Reds. It was a June game at the "friendly confines" of Wrigley Field. The vines on the outfield walls, the old score board, and the ambiance of one of the last remnants of old classic baseball stadiums. I was excited to say the least. I didn't even mind that I would share this experience with thousands of fans, in what is known as the World's Largest Beer Garden. Of course in Chicago land we have a saying, "If you don't like the weather, stick around, it'll change." This can have a dramatic impact on event planning.

As fate would have it, the day we went was the hottest day in June on record and humidity that matched. Over 500 people died that week in Chicago of heat exposure. There we were nine rows behind the first base dugout with great seats that just happened to put us in the only unshaded section of the stadium. My son Tom was about three years old and my wife Diane had brought a cooler of ice and towels hoping we could make through it the whole game.

I wanted some pictures to commemorate the Wrigley experience so I took Tom down to the first base dugout and sat him on top of it for a quick picture. Within seconds of his bottom touching that dugout he starts to scream and cry. I didn't think about the black tar roof on top of the structure, but it must have been 250 degrees! I felt horrible as I grabbed him as fast as I could, running back to momma to get an ice cold towel for his hot little fanny. What a Dad, huh? Brutal!

You know, it should have been a great family experience, but we left totally defeated after the second inning, soaked with a combination of sweat and ice towels. A miserable memory.

What should have been a fantastic family experience turned into a crash and burn scenario. Looking back at it, there only seemed to be a risk of bad weather and you never know weeks in advance what the weather will be. You can have an idea or forecast or trend, but never certainty. Only risk!

Red Money Investing

Red Money investing relies on forecasts, past correlations, analytical studies, common sense, and a little luck. If you are counting on fair weather, you may just get a hurricane instead. Red Money investing is where the weather of risk changes constantly. Column C is the only place where the clouds of market risk could blow in or the unseasonable heat and humidity of volatility might flare up. So, if we're going to use risk-oriented assets let's consider first a few ways the industry forecasts risk and then move on to some Red Money Strategies.

When investing in Column C it would be wise to take a profile test to see what type of risk tolerance you really have and determine the time frame for the money to be in this category. Most financial planners have questionnaires to help you determine risk tolerance. They should also help you determine your investing goals which will illuminate a time frame for the money you want invested. If you would like to take a test before seeing an advisor there is one available in Appendix Three.

Systematic Risk, Volatility, & Variance
(Now there's a mouthful!)

Wall Street is well known for using terms the average American doesn't understand. I'm not sure why this is the case; I just know it is what it is. I'm also pretty sure that even Wall Street doesn't understand what they're doing part of the time. This is witnessed by the "credit-default swap" debacle of 2008, which brought down giants like Bear Stearns and Lehman Brothers.

Yet, it is important to have a working knowledge of the basic terms used when investing Red Risk Money. If you don't understand, you might end up one day "un-retired" or extending your employment longer than you had planned. So, let's start with a few words you might have heard a broker say or an analyst use on a financial program. I'm probably half crazy for attempting what has never been done before; simplifying Wall Street jargon, but I'll give it the old college try.

First, when I say "the market" I'm referring to either the stock market or bond market as a whole. The stock market may be represented by an index such as the S&P 500 and the bond market by the Barclays Capital Aggregate Bond Index. The stock market is sometimes referred to as the equity markets where the average person can own a piece of the store. The bond market, which is the larger of the two, is where debt obligations are sold. A debt obligation is a note issued by an entity such as a corporation or governing body. The bond is guaranteed by the issuer who promises to pay interest on a regular basis. Thus we have stock-type risk and bond-type risk—two aspects of risk in the market as a whole.

Indexes like the S&P 500, Dow Jones Industrials, Russell 2000, Barclays Aggregate Bond Index to name a few, are used to measure the changes in the financial markets. Indexes are referred to as benchmarks against which mutual funds and other investments are measured. They use a theoretical portfolio of assets that are relative to the financial market or economy being measured. You can't actually invest in an index, but index mutual funds, futures and exchange traded funds are used by investors who want to buy into the market as a whole or a particular segment of the market.

Wall Street calls the risk or uncertainty associated with the entire market, or an entire segment of a market, "systematic risk." (1) In other words, investing in the market in general is uncertain all the time. There is never a point at which you can say you know where the market is headed. In fact, systematic risk implies that uncertainty is deep-seated in the market which moves up and down with regularity that cannot be anticipated. If you're a conservative investor, systematic risk gives you the runs!

How Wall Street measures risk associated with the market is through "volatility." People who study the market look at historical returns of a stock or index and plot them on a graph. They look to see how the dots on the graph relate to each other over time and in relationship to historical events. The further apart the dots on the graph, the higher the volatility. The higher the volatility, the riskier the investment.

Wall Street uses "variance" to describe the difference between where the returns are from an average return of the same asset or a corresponding index. So, if you took the monthly prices of a stock over a three-year period and plotted them on a graph you could see either how close together they are or how far apart they are. The further apart they are, the more volatile the stock is. How far they vary from the average price of the three years is called the variance. Blah, blah, blah.... It's deeply-rooted uncertainty! Get it?

Beta, R-Squared, and Standard Deviation

If volatility and variance are hard to understand, the next three are much easier.

Take *Beta* for instance. No, it's not that old video tape you have in your closet and were hoping would be valuable one day. Beta is a measure of risk or volatility as it relates to an index. Let's say a mutual fund you own has a Beta of 1 to the S&P 500 Index. This fund would then tend to go up about the same as the S&P and down about the same. If the Beta was 1.5, the fund would be 50% more volatile than the S&P. If the Beta was .5 then the fund would be 50% less volatile than the S&P.

Alpha, another well-used Wall Street term, is used to measure how much the fund's performance is better than the correlated benchmark index. If the fund's Alpha is 5, it outperformed its benchmark index by 5%. Fund managers are always trying to increase their Alpha or the degree in which they add value to your investment!

Standard Deviation is the "wobble factor", showing us how much a fund wobbles back and forth from its average return. The more it wobbles, the higher the risk.

Technically, Standard Deviation measures how a fund's performance over time is different from its average return. (2) The greater the difference, the higher the volatility. The higher the volatility, the more uncertainty in future returns. Uncertainty equals risk in which the conservative investor longs to minimize. If an investment has a high number here it is sure to be avoided by most conservative investors.

My friend Navi Dowty tells me professional traders look at the Standard Deviation more as a speedometer than a crystal ball. He says, "When the daily standard deviations are increasing, there is generally more fear in the markets, and thus more potential risk. The most common manifestation of the measurements of the standard deviation in real time is called the "VIX." The "VIX" is a measurement of the implied volatility of how the options that are used to protect portfolios are being priced in real time by traders in the S&P 500 markets." Navi is a Chartered Financial Analyst and I am sure he understands what all that means. I just think it means when the VIX is high it's time to buy, and when the VIX is low it's time to go.

The VIX is the Chicago Board Options Exchange ticker symbol for the Volatility Index which shows the markets 30-day expectations of volatility in the S&P 500. It is widely used by professional money managers and, while I believe it to be more useful than watching the DOW or the S&P, I am also sure it is not a derivative…of my last name.

R-Squared is interesting because it is the assessor of measurements. This measurement grades the accuracy of the assets movements that can be related to a benchmark index. If the grade is low, 70 or less, the Beta is probably not reliable. If the grade is higher than 85, the Beta might be considered to be more dependable. R-Squared sheds light on the veracity of risk measurements.(3)

There you have it. Wall Street jargon simplified. (Did it work?)

Stock Type Risk vs. Bond Type Risk

For conservative investors, the question for Column C is not only how much risk you want to take, but what type of risk and when to take it. While there are many choices that investors have, for the conservative, it's a simple choice between stock-type risk and bond-type risk. No credit-swaps, options, margins, or shorting the market for us. It's plain and simple.

So, the question for Column C Red Risk Money is this: what percent of your Red Risk Money do you want in stock-type risk and what percent do you want in bond-type risk? It is perfectly okay to have all of one and none of the other, or a simple 50% portion of each. It's up to your comfort level. Some of my clients over the years have wanted no stock-type risk whatsoever. That's fine. If you feel uncomfortable with money in equities, then don't be pressured into it.

I also have a rule for Red Risk Money that unless you have over two million dollars in investible assets, you probably want to stay away from individual stocks. I'm not talking about the stock your company gave you or stock inherited from your father. Individual stocks concentrate the risk on a single company rather than spreading the risk over many companies or markets. Unless you are very market savvy, you don't want in this game as a conservative investor.

I know some brokers will be reading this and saying, "Trust me, the weather will be just fine. I'm here to guide you." The point is not whether you can trust a broker's ability to pick stocks. The reason I don't believe you want to get into individual stocks is simple: risk is concentrated into one stock or a bundle of maybe 30 to 50 stocks if you have a manager. I believe the better route for the conservative investor is to spread the risk around with mutual funds or Exchange Traded Funds (ETF's). A mutual fund may have 30 to 150 stocks in it and you might own 10-12 funds which would spread the risk between 300 to 1500 different companies.

I also believe that, for the most part, owning individual bonds does the same thing to the bond-type risk that owning individual stocks does to the stock-type risk category. While using bond funds doesn't give you the potential to get your principal back at the end of the term, it can spread the bond risk around between many different bonds and types of bonds.

However, there is a significant disadvantage to bond funds. Since bonds can lose value in a rising interest rate climate, owning an individual bond that has an end at which time you can redeem your principal might be a good option for bond-type risk in Column C. The problem with individual bonds is the quality of the company issuing the bond. If you bought Enron or Bear Stearns bonds, you could have lost money. I actually think that a tactically managed account of bond funds is the best approach in bond-type risk for the conservative investor.

In the end I like the ability of a tactical manager to move in and out of different types of bond funds and money markets and potentially avoiding the nasty decline in a rising interest rate bond market. So, go tactical here.

One last thought on Bonds. Navi tells me bonds should be used when interest rates are high, not low. He says there hasn't been much talk about the risk in bonds in recent years because we have been on a long term decline in interest rates. That decline may be at an end, unless you think the interest rates can go down even further. Navi tells me if you want to see the real monster of bond risk, look back at the 1970's, the last time we had dramatically increasing interest rates and inflation. Many long-term bonds had their market prices cut in half by 1981 and 1982. We can't predict when interest rates and inflation will rise, but if history is any guide, it will happen. Then bond market prices will drop.

There is a huge amount of money in the bond market currently and some predict a bond market crash. The resounding noise of a bond market crash is much louder than a stock market crash. So, again I think tactical management here is the best move.

Who Chooses the Assets?

Choosing what specific assets go into the Red Risk Money strategies can be a daunting task for the average investor. That is why I suggest you get some help with this area. I believe that finding a good Registered Investment Advisor who charges a fee for asset management might be the optimal choice here. The reason is if you don't know anything about mutual funds, whether they are stock or bond related, you will have a hard time maximizing the potential of this area. I'm a bottom-line type who believes paying a fee for a good service is better than losing money because I'm too cheap.

However, I believe brokers from large broker dealers represent the same old Wall Street mentality. They are very predictable in what they recommend. Usually some well-known family of funds like American Funds, T. Rowe Price, ING, Fidelity, or proprietary funds, are used along with a smattering of bonds and a variable annuity or two. It is a commission-driven model. Commissions paid on trading stocks or mutual funds are so low they are not a consideration anymore. The real money is made for brokers in the shares of mutual funds and commissions on variable annuities. These assets can provide both immediate and ongoing commissions.

If you have a good amount of knowledge about mutual funds you might want to give it a try. By the way, if you have a good knowledge of mutual funds, my experience tells me you are really a moderate risk investor. No problem here, but we are most concerned about the conservative investor with little or no knowledge of mutual funds. They really shouldn't be trying to choose which fund or sector of funds to purchase. They don't know how to weigh each sector, and when to re-adjust the portfolio. Any of these decisions should be left to a professional who knows the territory and has a proven track record.

When choosing someone to manage your Red Risk Money, whether you choose a Registered Investment Advisor or a broker, it's important to find out how long they have been managing. You would also want to know their management "style;" what is the system they use to determine their investments, do they have a proven specialty, and what is their track record? Most importantly you want to know how they manage risk. I'm pretty sure you wouldn't want a recent college graduate with a lot of great ideas about investing to be the one deciding your fund choices.

Tactical vs. Buy & Hold Management

There are two styles of management that you might choose from: tactical or "buy & hold." Simply put, tactical management is active, daily management. In a "buy & hold" style, the manager chooses the sectors of the market, how much to weight each sector and then uses the best fund managers available. So in essence, the advisor is trying to choose an all-star team of managers and let them do the buying and selling of assets inside the funds. There is typically much less trading of mutual funds in an account with this style.

Choosing an all-star team of fund managers can be great when the all-star is riding a winning streak. But when the streak ends, it can be ugly. For instance, in 2007 an all-star fund favorite was Ken Heebner and the CGM Focus fund, which returned 79.97% for the year. But in 2008, Heebner gave back -48.18% and then under-performed the market in 2009 with a 10.42% return.(4) Take a look at what that meant for you, the investor.

$1,000 in CGM Focus Fund (CGMFX):

01-10-2007	$1,000
12-31-2007	$1,800
12-31-2008	$933
12-31-2009	$1,030

*(*Returns based on YahooFinance data)*

For a conservative investor, the above numbers are just too volatile. Yes, you were ahead of the game by the end of 2009, but the road to get there was far too bumpy. Besides, if you were like the average investor who pulls out when the market is down, you would never have recovered your $1,000 in 2009, as you sat on the sidelines licking your wounds.

The vaunted American Funds Growth Fund of America, used by many commissioned based brokers, was not any better. (5)

$1,000 in American Funds Growth Fund of America (AGTHX):

01-10-2007	$1,000
12-31-2007	$1,110
12-31-2008	$676
12-31-2009	$909

*(*Returns based on YahooFinance data)*

Not only was the road bumpy, but you lost some luggage in the end. So, choosing an all-star team of fund managers and sitting on them while you pay fees or commissions can be frustrating. "Buy & hold" is definitely a more growth-oriented risk tolerance management style.

However, a more tactical management style can yield some surprising results. The first plus for a tactical management style is its daily nature. Tactical managers seek to find returns by moving in and out of markets or segments of the market to take advantage of anomalies and strengths in certain market sectors depending on what they see in their analytical research and forecasts. They can be "all in" or "all out" on any given day.

Generally speaking, tactical managers choose a broad category such as equity growth and watch trends in that segment of the market to determine if they want to be in or out. At its best, it is done with a pre-determined process or model that dictates whether the manager buys, sells, or holds his position. A manager pulls the buy/sell trigger, but the process should determine the decision he makes, not his emotions.

Tactical management is the wave of the future because it is information driven and the investing world travels at the speed of the internet. It is a completely different world than it was even ten years ago and the future will probably be ruled by tactical managers. Appendix Four has articles from Bryce Kommerstad, Chief Investment Strategist of Redhawk Wealth Advisors, and Dan Hunt, Founder and President of Redhawk, which is a Registered Investment Advisor I use for my own practice. Bryce and Dan have created an incredible tactical management model with technology that is constantly on the cutting edge. So, check out their articles.Kommerstad

Again, Column C Red Money Investing is where the risk is in the ABC Model. You can choose stock-type risk or bond-type risk, and how much you want in either category. Finding a good money manager to help you implement your Red Money Strategy is somewhat like finding a good weatherman. Though they're not always right, they can often keep us from getting burned in the heat of a bear market.

- Nine -

What if it Happened Again?

A Negative Neighbor

I used to have a neighbor who was incredibly negative. There was nothing I could ever do right. He always complained. Have you ever had a neighbor like that? I mean, I could mow his lawn for him while he was on vacation, he would come back knock on my door, and tell me I had missed a spot! Now that's discouraging.

I thought I would teach him a lesson. I knew he loved duck hunting so I bought a hunting dog and trained it to walk on water. It was hard, but truly a smart dog. Next, I took my neighbor duck hunting. Sure enough my neighbor shot a duck and I yelled, "Fetch Bandit, Fetch!" Bandit jumped out of the boat, ran right on top of the water, fetched the duck and climbed back in the boat. Only the pads of his paws were damp when he dropped the duck at my neighbor's feet.

Totally unimpressed, my neighbor leaned back with his arms folded across his barrel chest as he grimaced and shook his head saying, "Darn dog can't swim can he?"

Now that's negative. You know the guy?

Okay, I stretched the truth about the dog...and the neighbor, but the point is some people can appear incredibly negative. Not me, though. Uh-uh. No way. I'm really a positive guy, but let me ask you a question.

What if the worst bear market in history happened again?

I know what you are thinking, "Man, this guys a real pessimist!" I got it. Yet, those who know me know I am a very real optimist and rarely believe the worst is going to happen. On the other hand, what if it did? What would the worst bear market in history do to your portfolio, which carries with it your lifestyle in retirement?

What was the worst bear market in history you ask? Most would argue the worst bear market started with the Crash of 1929 and didn't recover from its market high, until the fall of 1954 a 25-year bear. Okay, that's negative!

It is generally accepted that a bear market is a 20% drop in the broad market indexes such as the Dow Jones Industrial Average or the S&P 500 over a two month period. Bear markets are a time of deep pessimism, falling stock prices, and usually high volatility. A bear is not to be confused with a correction. The correction is usually a short period of time, something less than two months, while a bear market is two months or longer. (1)

There were two very large and very long bear markets in the twentieth century. As I previously mentioned the 1929 crash which lasted to 1954, and then the 1965-1982 bear market. Most seniors remember both and boomers definitely remember the gas lines of the 70's bear market. Russell Napier in his book *The Anatomy of a Bear* says on average every three years there's a bear market, every eight years there's a stinker of a bear market, and big bears last an average of 17 years. Napier also says the bear market that started in 2000 wouldn't end until 2011-2014, probably closer to the latter, with the Dow at less than 5000.(2) Now that's negative!

Everyone knows the old investing axiom, "Buy Low, Sell High." Find the bottom of the bear and invest. Then sell at the height of the bull run, maximizing your gains. If you can do this you can retire wealthy beyond imagination. Sounds easy, but it is incredibly difficult. In fact, Napier's book is all about trying to find the historical commonalities that run through bear markets so you would be able to estimate when the bottom of the next bear is and invest.

John D. Rockefeller is reported to have said, "The way to make money is to buy when blood is running in the streets." (3) I believe this means you ought to buy when everyone else is selling and sell when everyone else is buying. Warren Buffett says, "We simply attempt to be fearful when others are greedy and to be greedy only when others are fearful." (4) Again, sounds like good advice, but how does the average investor know when everyone else is selling or buying. Isn't that just a guess anyway?

I believe this is where the ABC Model of Investing shines its brightest, because investing in the three categories will almost always increase opportunities for success in a long hard bear market. In fact, when others have lost money in a buy-and-hold mentality believing the market will recover over an extended period of time, those who have diversified in the ABC Model have made money.

Using the ten years of the market from 2000 through 2009 as an example, let's see how the ABC's would have performed. If Russell Napier and other economists are right, the current bear started with the tech-bubble bursting in 2000, this would be a good ten years to view. (5)

WHAT IF...? : S&P 500 LAST 10 YEARS

Investable Assets $500,000

Current Asset Allocation

2000 - 2009 S&P 500 Returns:	Interest A 3%	Cap B 7%	C S&P 500	Total	Dollar Gain/Loss	Percent Gain/Loss
	$50,000	**$0**	**$450,000**	**$500,000**		
-10.14%	$51,500	$0	$404,370	$455,870	-$44,130	-9%
-13.04%	$53,045	$0	$351,640	$404,685	-$51,185	-11%
-23.37%	$54,636	$0	$269,462	$324,098	-$80,587	-20%
26.38%	[illegible]	[illegible]	[illegible]	$396,821	$72,723	23%
8.99%	[illegible]	[illegible]	[illegible]	$429,125	$32,303	8%
3.00%	$59,703	$0	$382,296	$441,998	$12,874	4%
13.62%	$61,494	$0	$434,464	$495,858	$53,860	12%
3.53%	$63,339	$0	$449,698	$513,036	$17,178	3%
-38.49%	$65,239	$0	$276,609	$341,848	-$171,188	-34%
19.67%	$67,196	$0	$331,018	$398,214	$56,366	16%
Total After 10 Yrs:	**$67,196**	**$0**	**$331,018**	**$398,214**	-$101,786	-20%
Current %:	10%	$0	90%			

-$101,786

The illustration above shows the S&P 500 returns (6) for the years 2000 through 2009 on the left. The investible assets are $500,000. This example shows a typical investor who has about 10% in cash earning an average of 3% and 90% allocated to the market represented by the S&P 500. We use the broad market index to approximate what investing in the market in general was like over that period of time. Certainly an investor could have been in more or less risk than illustrated here. Yet, the illustration shows in general terms how the market performed from 2000-2009. Notice, there are no monies allocated to Column B, which are Index Annuities.

The chart shows at the end of the ten-year period, this investor would have lost over $100,000. I don't know about you, but a 20% loss in the market is devastating when it comes to retirement!* Imagine if you were 52 years old in 2000 and planning to retire when most people retire at age 62. Would you do what many have had to do, which is work another 3-5 years in hopes of recovering those assets needed to retire?

And what if it happens again? What if the next ten years aren't any better than the last ten years? Can you afford to lose another 20% or possibly more? Can you continue to push off your retirement indefinitely?

When I show this graph to clients they tell me, "Yep, that's about what happened to us." Yet, the same clients will surprisingly stay in this broken down Wall Street model attempting to recover with a hope and a prayer.

There has to be a better way, and I believe there is. Look at the graph below.

WHAT IF...? : S&P 500 LAST 10 YEARS

Current Asset Allocation

2000 - 2009 S&P 500 Returns:	Interest A 3%	Cap B 7%	C S&P 500	Total	Dollar Gain/Loss	Percent Gain/Loss
	$50,000	$300,000	$150,000	$500,000		
-10.14%	$51,500	$300,000	$134,790	$486,290	-$13,710	-3%
-13.04%	$53,045	$300,000	$117,213	$470,258	-$16,032	-3%
-23.37%	$54,636	$300,000	$89,821	$444,457	-$25,801	-5%
26.38%	$56,275	$321,000	$113,515	$490,791	$46,334	10%
8.99%	$			$525,154	$34,363	7%
3.00%	$			$540,909	$15,755	3%
13.62%	$			$584,820	$43,911	8%
3.53%	$63,339	$391,901	$149,899	$605,138	$20,318	3%
-38.49%	$65,239	$391,901	$92,203	$549,342	-$55,796	-9%
19.67%	$67,196	$419,334	$110,339	$596,869	$47,427	9%
Total After 10 Yrs:	$67,196	$419,334	$110,339	$596,869	$96,869	19%
Desired %:	10%	60%	30%			

$198,655
Difference

Using the same $500,000 over the identical ten years (7), let's allocate 60% to short-term laddered maturities in indexed annuities. Assuming an average index cap of 7% we begin to see how the ABC Model is a great model to use for bear markets. This time period was a bear market and yet the allocation made $96,869 over the same time period while the first example lost $101,786. That's a difference of $198,655 over a really nasty decade. It's probably the difference between you retiring when you want to or not!

"The first rule is not to lose.
The second rule is not to forget the first rule."
Warren Buffett ***(8)***

Mr. Buffet helps us to understand why the ABC Model works so well. The key is simply to protect your principal and retain your gains. Remember Green Money Rules #1 and #2? That's right. Green Money Rule #1 is the same as the first rule for Warren Buffet. Don't lose! Look at the Red Column C in the years 2000 through 2002. You started with $150,000 in 2000 and ended with $89,000. Remember the "Tech-Bubble?" If you were invested in tech-stocks in those years you took a much greater beating. Now look at the same years in the Green

Column B. You started with $300,000 and ended with $300,000. Are you happy? Darn right! You didn't gain anything, but you didn't LOSE anything. Zero is your Hero!

Look down the Red Money Column at the ninth year, 2008, and the loss of 38%. It took you five years to just about get back to where you started in 2000 and then the bottom dropped out. You lost $55,796 and only had $92,203 left of your Red Risk money. Yet, peer into the ninth year of the Green Money Column and notice you didn't lose a dime and have $391,901* which is more money than you started with in the year 2000. Can't say the same for the Red Risk Column can you?

I'm not saying that you shouldn't invest in the market, but I am saying you can diversify with Fixed Principal Assets like laddered maturities of Fixed Indexed Annuities and the decade wouldn't have been the abysmal lost decade of 2000 through 2009.

The decade from 2010 and forward doesn't look any better either. With government bailouts, increasing mortgage defaults, escalating taxes, a new government controlled health care system, and a fifteen trillion dollar rising deficit, something is going to get ugly. I hate to think it's your retirement account in the market that gets devastated.

I know. It's negative. But what if it happened again?

**Disclosure: Past performance is no guarantee future results. Example uses a 7% cap and assumes no dollars withdrawn from accounts. Crediting rates including caps for FIA's can change and are determined by the insurance companies at the time of issue. Annuities carry surrender penalties for early withdrawal. Future performance cannot be predicted or guaranteed. FIA's are not registered as a security with the SEC and is not invested directly in any stock, bond, or security investment. FIA products, features, and benefits vary by state. Annuities are guaranteed by the claims paying ability of the issuing insurance carrier.*

- Ten -

The Cowboy Preacher

Richard F. Vick: The Cowboy Preacher

My grandfather, Richard F. Vick, was born to a hardworking Danish immigrant family in Minnesota on April 16th, 1892. He grew up to be a rugged, adventurous young man who tried his hand at cow-poking and loved it. He got married and was called into the ministry, becoming a circuit-riding Methodist preacher in the harsh environment of eastern Montana. Once he had five churches he pastored at the same time. In our family, we referred to him as the "Cowboy Preacher."

My dad would tell stories of living in the church parsonage. No electricity. No running water. No "facilities" inside the house. He said the winter blizzards in eastern Montana were so bad that in order to use the "facilities" they went outside and grabbed onto a frozen rope that led them to the outhouse. He would really get angry when, after braving the blizzard and making it to the shed, someone had used the last page of the Sears catalog. I can't even imagine it. Life was so different then.

Life changes and times change. My grandfather never really had a concept of retirement. He worked hard as a cow-puncher, hard as a preacher, and when he was older, he used to be an interim pastor. The love of his life, wife Mildred, suffered from a brain tumor that took her life in 1969. He missed her terribly. He lost a son in the 70s and it almost crushed him. But, Grandpa was an incredibly strong man with an incredibly strong faith in an incredible God who had more for him to do. When he was too old to teach any more Bible studies and preach any more sermons, he retired to an assisted living facility in Bozeman, Montana. There he passed away in the fall of 1980. He was a great man. A truly great man! I loved him dearly.

The Biggest Need for Retirees: Income Planning

You know, that's how a lot of our grandparents were. They didn't really have a concept of retirement. They worked hard and when their eyes darkened, their backs weakened, and their hands couldn't grip anymore, they stopped working, sat down…and died.

The concept of retirement in America grew out of the reforms made in the great depression; the most significant of course was Social Security. In 1933, Congress passed the Social Security bill that enabled people who were age 65 to receive income checks monthly from the government starting in 1935. It was originally intended as a supplement to income for the elderly, yet has turned into the major source of income for many retirees. It is interesting to note the average retirement age in 1910 was 74 years old, and the average in 2006 was age 62. (1) This is most likely true because it is when people can begin to receive early Social Security.

It's interesting to note according to government actuarial tables a male age 62 is expected to live to just about 80 years old. If he reaches 75 he's expected to reach age 85, and if he reaches age 85 he's expected to live until age 90 plus. Women of those ages (never ask though) are expected to live another year and a half to two years longer than their male counter parts. (2) We are living longer and it is definitely putting pressure on finances, both personal and for the government as well. Imagine a government trying to fund retirement for millions and millions of Boomers over the next 30-50 years. Not just Social Security, but Medicare and Medicaid are headed for real trouble.

So, your job is trying to provide enough of an asset base to last through retirement. If you are retired, your job is to make the money last through retirement. Tough job! It seems like this should be easy. You make money, you save money, and you spend it in retirement. Simple, right? Not exactly.

We are talking about making money last for at least three decades. What lasts three decades anyway? Plastic water bottles? Marriage? Well, considering a divorce rate of over 50% and spouses that pass away prematurely during retirement, maybe not. These can be painful realities as we head into what is supposed to be our "Golden Years." The water bottle outlasts our marriage and our money. Something's not right here.

Still, life happens. And as I said, it happens for three decades on average in retirement. The highs and lows. The arthritis and dementia. The grandkids and poodles. Three decades of life all of which we have to fund. While there is so much more to enjoying retirement than money, if you screw up the money it has a dramatic impact on all the other aspects of those Golden Years. In fact, if you screw the money up you may have to go to work at the Golden Arches!

Here's another happy thought—inflation. Inflation relates to how effective your buying power will remain for the course of your retirement. Even with straight-line inflation figured at 3%, what costs a $1 today will cost $2.40 when the 62-year-old couple's last survivor reaches 90.

And what, may I ask, inflates at only 3% for retirees?

Medication? No.

Medical treatments? Wrong!

Senior housing? No way!

Long-term nursing care? Laughable!

All of the above expenses increase at a much faster rate than 3% annually.

What is the answer? Is risking principal in the stock market to chase 10%–12 % gains the answer? Certainly, in the past the market has been the place to beat inflation. In 1950 the S&P 500 ranged from 17 to 23. In 2010 the S&P fluctuated between 1,000 and 1,200. (3) Yes, more than 50 times what it was 60 years prior. That is fantastic considering we have had 13 bear markets in those 60 years…some dipping thirty percent or more!! So, on the surface at least, the risk is worth the reward.

What happens if the next 60 years doesn't play out like the last 60 years? Or the next 30 years like the last 30 years, or for that matter the next 10 years? Do you have 60 years to overcome losses? Absolutely not!

What's the answer? How do you plan for income that will last in the bearish of markets? One of the keys is knowing where you are in life. My grandfather was good at it. He was never lost, at least as far as life is concerned. When it comes to finances it's important to realize that you are in one of two stages, accumulation or distribution.

Accumulation vs. Distribution

Retirement happens in thirds. Let me explain. Remember, with life expectancies for couples in retirement lasting 20 to 30 years you have to fund retirement for three decades to be safe. We are living longer and it ain't gettin' cheaper! This makes it incredibly important to know the difference between investing for accumulation and investing for distribution, or better put, when you are accumulating retirement funds (accumulation) and then when you will start to live off those funds (distribution).

To Illustrate, I have created a hypothetical 10-year market index. If you started in the first year with $500,000 and put that money in the sample index, at the end of 10 years you would have $631,205, assuming no withdrawals.

Let me ask you a question though. If you inverted the index over the same 10-year period of time, so the 10th year return would flip to be the first year return, the 9th year would be the second year return and so on would the final dollar amount be the same? Now, most people (including me) when first asked this question intuitively say "no." You would have to have a different number, right?

Wrong. The commutative principal of multiplication states that when multiplying numbers, you can put them in any order and the result will be the same (see illustration below).

Hypothetical Index
Beginning Value $500,000

Year	*Annual Return*	*End of Year Value*	*Inverse Return*	*End of Year Value*
1	28%	$640,000	-38%	$310,000
2	-10%	$576,000	-12%	$272,800
3	15%	$662,400	2%	$278,256
4	17%	$775,008	15%	$319,994
5	1%	$782,758	26%	$403,193
6	26%	$986,275	1%	$407,225
7	15%	$1,134,216	17%	$479,453
8	2%	$1,156,901	15%	$547,921
9	-12%	$1,018,073	-10%	$493,129
10	-38%	**$631,205**	28%	**$631,205**

That's right! You can put all the negative numbers at the beginning, middle, end, or scatter them throughout the years and you will end up with the same number each time! That is unless you take money out of the equation.

Let's say you start again in the first year with the same $500,000, use the same 10-year hypothetical index returns, yet this time take out an income stream for retirement. Let's take out $35,000 a year and use a 3% rate of inflation. So, each year we would see the withdrawal grow to cover rising expenses until in the 10th year the withdrawal is $45,667. If we use the same index returns we end up with $313,017. Not bad! It seems to really work.

Hypothetical Index
Beginning Value $500,000 Withdrawal $35,000 Inflation 3%

Year	*Annual Return*	*Annual Withdrawal*	*End of Year Value*
1	28%	$35,000	$605,000
2	-10%	$36,050	$508,450
3	15%	$37,132	$547,586
4	17%	$38,245	$602,430
5	1%	$39,393	$569,062
6	26%	$40,575	$676,443
7	15%	$41,792	$736,118

8	2%	$43,046	$707,795
9	-12%	$44,337	$578,522
10	-38%	**$45,667**	**$313,017**

However, if we invert the returns again, so year 10 is now year one and so on, we run out of money in year eleven! That's incredible isn't it? One way it works for 10 years, but simply invert the numbers as below, and you run out of money in ten years. If you are retired, you are headed back to work!

Hypothetical Index

Beginning Value $500,000 Withdrawal $35,000 Inflation 3%

Year	*Annual Return*	*Annual Withdrawal*	*End of Year Value*
1	-38%	$35,000	$275,000
2	-12%	$36,050	$205,950
3	2%	$37,132	$172,938
4	15%	$38,245	$160,633
5	26%	$39,393	$163,004
6	1%	$40,575	$124,060
7	17%	$41,792	$103,358
8	15%	$43,046	$75,816
9	-10%	$44,337	$23,898
10	28%	**$45,667**	**-$15,078**

Why does this happen? It's simple. The biggest losing year was the first year, followed by another losing year. In the first example, the first year was positive followed by a smaller loss.

You see the problem is we can't know when the losses will happen and how significant they will be. If it is true that we have to plan for three decades of retirement, not knowing when the losses will happen, means we have to plan very carefully. If you have big losses in the last 10 years you might have a chance, yet, if the big losses are in the first ten years it is devastating! You have totally blown your retirement.

Understanding you can't screw up the first decade of retirement, or any decade, and make your money last is an important concept. That's why the ABC Model is a logical alternative to Wall Street for the most conservative of investors. You can preserve principal, retain your gains, and even guarantee income.

There are many ways to guarantee income. Yet, guaranteeing income, principal, and gains at the same time is the magic of Fixed Indexed Annuities with Guaranteed Income Benefits, along with a well thought out strategy for each third of retirement.

Green Money Income Plans

The standard Wall Street model is to mix bonds and stocks in a portfolio and take an annual percentage out of the account, say 4% to 6%, for income and see if the account will last a lifetime. In other words, they hope the return is high enough to make the income last and they pray the inevitable bear market losses won't destroy their retirement dream. I tell clients, instead of hoping and praying an income plan will work, let's just guarantee it.

Remember Green Money Rule #3? Guarantee Your Income! One of the income plans that fit into the ABC Model is a concept called, "Split Annuity Income." This is the practice of creating income by putting part of the assets designated to create income into an immediate annuity, one that pays a monthly income right away and ending after a specified number of years. The left over part of the assets designated to create income is placed in a deferred annuity for growth which will be used to create an increase in income when the immediate annuity ends. Take a look at the following Split Annuity Illustration #1.

Split Annuity Illustration #1: Ten Year Split*

Beginning Value

$500,000

10 Year Income Bucket	**Growth Bucket**
Allotment: $215,000	Allotment: $285,000
Annual: $25,271	Bonus: 8%
Monthly: $2,106	LIBR: 6.5%

Annual Taxable Amount: $5,054 Years Deferred: 10
Value After 10 Years: $0

Beginning of 11th Year

Guaranteed Income Account Value (not cash): $577,783

11th Year Income by Guaranteed Withdrawals

- Ages 60 to 69 at 5%: $28,889
- Ages 70 to 79 at 6%: $34,667
- Ages 80 and up at 7%: $40,445

Illustration #1 shows the concept of a Ten-Year Split Annuity. In this illustration, we assume an example of $500,000 of investible assets allocated to create income in retirement. The left side of the illustration uses less than half the total amount designated for the plan, $215,000, in an immediate annuity for 10 years. It creates an income of $25,271 a year or $2,106 month. If the $215,000 is coming from after-tax monies, the tax benefits on the income are significant. Of the $25,271 a year of income, roughly $5,054 is taxable during the first ten years. *(All rates are assumed and income is estimated not actual. Actual rates will be those used at the time of annuitization with the specific insurance company chosen. The illustration is an estimate based on current annuitization tables.)*

Second, on the right side of the illustration we place the balance of the original amount, $285,000, in a Fixed Indexed Annuity offering an 8% bonus, and a Lifetime Income Benefit Rider (LIBR) of 6.5%. We let it grow for ten years, while the first annuity finishes paying out. The income rider increases the premium by the 8% bonus, and then calculates growth for income purposes by 6.5% each year. This is not cash growth, only a calculated benefit to determine income in the future. If the person owning this income plan is 65 to start with, his immediate income side will run out in ten years, depleting principal and interest over those ten years. Yet, the second half has a guaranteed income of $34,667 at age 75, an increase of over $9,000 a year of income.

The cash account created in the second bucket is still growing according to the index returns of the annuity, and is depleted as the income payments are taken out. It doesn't matter if the cash is depleted by low index returns and income leaving the account because the income is guaranteed for the rest of your life, no matter what happens to the cash value of the contract. Now that's powerful.

You could use the Ten Year Split Annuity as illustrated above or a Five Year Split Annuity (Illustration 2) which allows for more diversity in the plan giving the retiree a chance to change the plan in five years rather than ten years. In the Five-Year Split you only use $122,620 in the immediate annuity that pays the same $25,271 a year, but for five years instead of ten. Using the balance of $377,380 in another annuity with an 8% bonus creates a guaranteed income of $33,504 at age 70, over an $8,000 a year increase. Remember the $33,504 is guaranteed for the rest of your life, no matter what happens to the cash in the account due to any lean years in the market where the index credits would be low. Guarantees, or a hope and a prayer. Not much of a decision to make.

Split Annuity Illustration #2: Five Year Split*

Beginning Value

$500,000

5 Year Income Bucket	**Growth Bucket**
Allotment: $122,620	Allotment: $377,380
Annual: $25,271	Bonus: 8%
Monthly: $2,106	LIBR: 6.5%
Annual Taxable Amount: $4,549	Years Deferred: 5
Value After 5 Years: $0	

Beginning of 6th Year

Guaranteed Income Account Value (not cash): $558,407

11th Year Income by Guaranteed Withdrawals

- Ages 60 to 69 at 5%: $27,920
- Ages 70 to 79 at 6%: $33,504

- Ages 80 and up at 7%: $39,088

Guaranteeing income using ABC-Model strategies creates some freedom in retirement lifestyles—freedom and security. Like I said, if you screw up the first third of retirement, it affects so many other facets that make a fulfilling retirement. Hoping and praying the market won't take a downturn and swallow your money whole along with your dreams of the "Golden Years" is not a solution. Green Money Guarantees are the solution.

I think my grandfather would have loved to have the option to retire at age 62. I think he would have been impressed by the guarantees. I think he might have chosen to continue his Kingdom work well into his "retirement," but with some creative choices—maybe a ranching ministry in eastern Montana to some wayward Cowboys. He would have loved it.

**This information is not intended to give tax, legal, or investment advice. Please seek advice from a qualified professional on these matters. Annuity Contracts are products of the insurance industry and are not guaranteed by any bank or insured by the FDIC. When purchasing a fixed indexed annuity, you own an annuity contract backed by the insurance company, you are not purchasing shares of stocks or indexes. Product features such as interest rates, caps, and participation rates may vary by product and state and may be subject to change. Surrender charges may apply for early withdrawals. Be sure to review the specific product disclosure for more details. Guarantees are based on the financial strength and claims paying ability of the insurance company.*

Lifetime income benefit riders are used to calculate lifetime payments only. The income account value is not available for cash surrender or in a death benefit. Excess withdrawals may reduce lifetime income and may incur surrender charges. Fees may apply. Guarantees based on the financial strength and claims paying ability of the insurance company. See specific product disclosure for more details.

- Eleven -

I Should Have Listened

Remodeling Horrors

Mike warned me. He told me, "If you are going to remodel your house, find a good contractor you trust and move out 'till he's done." I should have listened because he was just one of many people warning me of the horrors of remodeling. I told him it would be over in six weeks. The contractor promised. He said seven weeks at the outside.

To his credit, even the contractor warned me once you start tearing into 20-year-old walls, you never know what you are going to find. Air ducts and electrical pipes that just shouldn't be there delay and re-route the best laid plans.

I should have listened.

As I'm writing this chapter, we are thirteen weeks in to the project and hoping the fourteenth week will see the end. Unbelievable! I had so many plans for this summer that have been either put on the back burner or scorched all together because of this monstrous project. The kitchen, family room, foyer, dining area, sun room, powder room, wood floors, and stairs to the second floor, are being totally re-done. Granted they look beautiful. I never thought "Golden Beach" granite counter tops could look so magnificent. Add to that the wonder of travertine backsplashes, a stone sink, and angel white cabinets. Awe-inspiring!

But, I should have listened.

It's not so much that the cabinets sat in our garage for two weeks while the contractor was busy on "other" jobs. Okay, it was that plus the dirt and dust covering everything in the garage and inside the house. I mean everywhere! They sanded the wood floors, trim, stairs, dry wall and anything else they could find to sand. They sawed and sawed and sawed (I think my lungs are full of wood chips). When the granite installers banged into the new decorative oven hood so hard that it not only gouged the hood, but broke off a piece of the most beautiful granite on the planet, I knew I was close to the end. My wife and I were nearly in tears. Truth is we were an emotional mess long before the granite. I imagined myself in a shaking huddled mass on the new wood floors, curled up in the fetal position with my thumb in my mouth.

I really should have listened.

401(k) Plan: Remodel or Replace

Don't get me wrong. I'm not going to suggest that your 401(k) is in need of repair. It is what it is and you can't do a thing about it until you get out of it. Actually, it's not just in need of repair or remodeling. If you are in retirement or close to it, you will probably want to replace it. A 401(k) plan is a great place to be while you're employed, but once you retire or maybe a little before, it's time to get out. You are probably wondering what could possibly go wrong with a 401(k). I know, I know…as Desi Arnez used to say, "Lucy, you got some 'splainin' to do!"

Some 'Splainin"

In 1978, the US Internal Revenue Code was remodeled to add section 401(k), which allowed employees to defer a part of their income into personal savings accounts. Monies deposited in the account are not included as income in the year they were deducted and not taxed until income is taken out. By 2003, 438,000 companies had developed 401(k) plans and by 2007, Americans had $3 trillion dollars invested in 401(k) plans. *(1)(2)*

With so many American Boomers retiring with 401(k) plans, it's important to discuss what to do with a plan once you retire. While you are still working, and especially if your employer is matching your deposits or part of your deposits, a

401(k) plan is a great place to be. Once you retire, though, there are some better options. There are even pre-retirement options available. Let's take a look at seven possible problems with 401(k) plans and why you should do a little remodeling of your retirement assets.

Seven Problems with Your 401(k)

Problem #1: Is Your 401k Compliant?

Is your employer or former employer's 401k plan compliant? Will it stay compliant throughout your retirement years? You would think this is an "automatic yes," but apparently not. The IRS on its website has some enlightening information as it relates to plans that go bad.

It appears that beginning in 2002, the IRS started to examine Form 5500 returns for 401(k) plans in various geographical areas throughout the country. They analyzed these returns and identified issues in detail.

"The issues identified in the examination of 401(k) plans within the various market segments mirrored those identified in 401(k) plans as a whole. The cause of these errors varied from case-to-case. However, the overwhelming identified cause of an error occurring in 401(k) plans within the completed market segments was the Failure to Follow the Terms of the Plan." (3)

The rather astounding discovery of the IRS analysis was that the employer failed to follow the rules of its own plan documents. The IRS even lists the top ten reasons for plan failure right on their website.(4) Of course we all know that trying to follow the IRS and its details is akin to nailing Jell-O to a wall, but these are professionals who make the mistakes, not amateurs.

While I am confident all the details of your 401(k) plan are given the attention they deserve, there is still the outside possibility they aren't or the IRS Website would not be listing the top reasons for plan failures. The question is how do you know your company is following the rules? Do you simply trust your company as most do? It would seem important for a successful retirement that your assets reside in a secure environment where they are free from the kind of exposure listed on the IRS Website. The reason is simple: failure of a 401(k) plan triggers total taxation of plan benefits for everyone in the plan!

Granted, this doesn't happen often because the IRS will allow the sponsoring company a certain amount of leeway to make corrections. Yet, I can't help thinking of all the broken pension promises over the years from highly reputable companies who cut benefits for retirees because they messed up the pension fund. It's just a thought. Maybe pulling money out of your 401(k) and taking control of it before somebody at the home office screws up the accounting might make sense.

Otherwise, you might be saying, "I should have listened."

Problem #2: Roth accounts in a 401(k) have issues.

A Roth opened inside a 401(k) account is referred to as a DRAC, a **D**esignated **R**etirement **Ac**count, and has to follow a different set of rules than a normal Roth IRA.

Typically Roth IRA's provide an excellent vehicle for those saving for retirement and those already retired who want tax advantaged income. There can be no better tax advantage than tax-free income and that's what a Roth IRA provides. Monies deposited in a Roth IRA are tax-free once the account has passed it's "non-exclusion" period of 5 years. Money can be withdrawn prior to the five years on a FIFO (First In, First Out) basis, which simply means your principal is taken out first. Yet after the 5-year period, all monies withdrawn are tax free.(5)

The IRS also considers the Roth beginning date for any Roth contributions as January 1st of the year in which the account was opened. For example, if you opened a Roth on November 15th of 2010, the start date of the "non-exclusion" period would be January 1st of 2010. The client could then start taking tax-free withdrawals from the account January 1st, 2015. Opening a contributory Roth account begins the 5-year "non-exclusion" period for all ensuing Roth accounts, unless they're in a 401(k). If a Roth is a DRAC, then each new Roth opened inside other 401(k) plans with subsequent employers start a new 5-year period before tax-free money can be withdrawn.(6)

A Roth account inside a 401(k) plan is also subject to the same rules as the 401(k) plan. There is one rule that is especially troublesome for a Roth inside a 401(k). A Roth inside a 401(k) is subject to the Required Minimum Distribution rules. In other words, you would be required to start taking income out of your Roth at age 70 and a half just like a regular IRA.(7) This is not true with a Roth outside a 401(k) plan.

The lifetime RMD rules can only be prevented by rolling the DRAC to a Roth IRA outside the 401(k) plan.

The DRAC 5-year non-exclusion period does not carry over to the new Roth IRA. Opening a Roth account, outside a DRAC will begin the 5 year "non-exclusion" period for all ensuing contributory Roth accounts opened at later dates, as Natalie Choate says in her book, *Life and Death Planning for Retirement Benefits*:

"The Five-Year Period (called in the statute the "non-exclusion period") for all of a participant's Roth IRAs begins on January 1 of the first year for which a contribution was made to any Roth IRA maintained for that participant."(8)

In other words, if a client opened a Roth on November 11th, 2010, the beginning date for figuring in the 5-year non-exclusion period for all other Roth accounts started after 2010 would then become January 1st, 2010. (9)

You might want to start a new Roth outside of your 401(k) to begin a five-year "non-exclusion" period for future rollovers of DRAC's.

Problem #3: Limited Choices.

Surely one of the greatest problems with 401(k) plans are the limited investment choices, especially when it comes to conservative investing. While larger company plans offer a variety of mutual fund companies and a few money markets they pale in comparison to the universe of options available outside a 401(k). Smaller companies have even fewer choices, some with only one family of funds.

This is a conservative investor's nightmare when it comes to finding an asset that doesn't experience market losses. Remember Warren Buffet's first rule of investing? Don't lose any money! Rule number two? Never forget rule number one. When you look at your 401(k) plan with absolutely no options for protected assets and this is your primary retirement account, it's enough to start you looking for the barf bag in the back of the seat in front of you. No kidding!

If having no protected accounts wasn't bad enough, all you have to help you decide where to invest is a little booklet explaining the options. It lists the fund families, shows the returns of all the mutual funds, and explains the rules. You look around for help, and the Human Resource personnel are nice people, but they are not financial advisors. The broker may come to the offices once a year. Some companies are located in a different city than the broker who set up the plan and employees have no access to him.

Of course, the final insult is the limited ability to make changes within your plan. To do so you either have to go online, run through the website maze, or call a toll free number and fumble through the company's phone options. If by chance you finally land on the right option, you end up misplacing your PIN number and have to start all over again!

This is not good. This is not choice. This is a conservative investor's highway to insanity, much like a 14-week remodel job. (Did I mention I should have listened!?)

Problem #4: The 20% Withholding Trap.

Well, now we're making progress. You finally decide you want to get out of your 401(k) plan only to find out your company withheld 20% of your account, which you will have to pay the taxes on next year's return. Say what?

First you have to understand what a "distributive rollover" is. You have probably heard you can receive money from a pre-tax dollar plan, put the money in your account and have 60 days to find a new plan and deposit the assets. That is called a distributive rollover because they distributed the money to you. However, with 401(k) plans the IRS rules require the plan to withhold (for federal tax) 20%. NO EXCEPTIONS! Since you don't receive the 20%, it is taxed at the end of the year as a distribution. Not only that, but you can only rollover once every 12 months.

So, here's the No Tax Distribution plan or how to avoid the 20% trap. Don't have the company make the check out to you, but rather have the plan make the check out to the company you want to invest with. Make use of what's called a "Trustee-to-Trustee Transfer." You never see the check; it is sent directly to the next company. No withholding.

In some instances, a plan will make the check out to the new company, but send it to you. Don't worry, this won't trigger any withholding. Simply forward the check on to the company you want to invest with.

The 20% Withholding Trap is easily avoided if you follow the rules. Using a professional is often helpful in these matters. (Make sure he's a financial professional and not a contractor.)

Problem #5: Limited Beneficiary Options.

Don't take this wrong, but if your spouse is the only option listed on your 401(k), it's a bad thing. This is one of the more distressing items on the list. Most people would like the money in their plan to go to their spouse, but what happens if you and your spouse die in a tragic remodeling accident? (It could happen). Where does the money go? I'm sure the state you live in has planned for this, but I'm pretty confident you would not want the state to control this decision. The problem is many plans only have one place for a beneficiary or the participant never filled out a beneficiary form.

To solve this problem, check your beneficiary designations on your plan to make sure you have listed at least one person to receive your money—other than the state of course. You would be surprised at how many people have missed this step completely and die with no beneficiaries listed.

I would suggest you conduct a beneficiary review with a financial professional or legal counsel. They can run through your beneficiary options with you. It's important to not only list a primary beneficiary, but also "contingent" and "tertiary" beneficiaries. A primary beneficiary receives all the Plan assets when you pass away. If you and your primary beneficiary pass away together in a car accident (sorry), your listed "contingent" beneficiary or beneficiaries would inherit plan assets. Generally, you list your spouse as a primary beneficiary, followed by your children. You might have one primary and three contingent beneficiaries. The most common way to list contingent beneficiaries are by percentages. Just remember that the percentages have to add up to 100%.

You can also list "tertiary" beneficiaries, which are people who receive plan assets if you and your contingent beneficiaries die in a plane crash on your way to a family vacation, (again, sorry). That would mean you and your immediate family was most likely taken out of the inheritance picture. Then, you might want to list grandchildren, nieces, nephews, brothers, sisters, or parents.

Tertiary beneficiaries can be used in many ways to pass on assets in complex estate plans to help with taxation. If you don't think of it ahead of time, your children won't have helpful options come tax time. For instance, if one of your children wanted to "disclaim" their share of the inheritance and let their kids, your grandchildren, inherit the plan assets so they could avoid a heavy tax, you would have to plan out the option in advance.

Think of it this way. Primary beneficiaries are first level inheritors; contingent beneficiaries are second level inheritors; and tertiary beneficiaries are third level inheritors.

You can see that a "beneficiary review" of your plan might be in order. One of the details you may discover about your 401(k) plan is that it doesn't provide for the any of the above listed options. That would simply be another reason to rollover your plan into an IRA where you can have exactly what you want to happen upon your demise a certainty.

You don't want to end up at death saying, "I should have listened." Well, that's a stretch, but you get the idea.

Problem #6: Required Minimum Distribution Errors.

Let me ask you a question. Say, you are retired and have an IRA worth $250,000, a 401(k) worth $100,000, and a 403(b) worth $125,000, are 71 years old, and are planning to take your Required Minimum Distribution (RMD). Can you withdraw an amount from just your 401(k) plan sufficient to cover all three plans? Many people along with many advisors make the same mistake of saying "yes." That's correct. "Yes" is a wrong answer. You must take a Required Minimum Distribution from each type of plan. A 401(k) RMD cannot cover other qualified plan RMD requirements. This may well be the most common mistake made amongst plan holders.

Yet, if you were to hold three separate IRA's, you could take one Required Minimum Distribution from just one of the accounts sufficient to cover all three accounts. This would allow you to take a distribution from an underperforming asset leaving more money in better performing assets. Imagine that kind of flexibility and you can imagine yourself out of your 401(k) plan, and into stronger options.

Are you listening?

Problem #7: 401(k)'s are the Non-Stretch Plan.

This could cost your heirs a million. A Stretch or Multi-Generational IRA plan is a plan in which your assets are passed to beneficiaries who leave them in the plan and simply take Required Minimum Distributions based on their IRS life expectancy tables. This allows the assets to grow tax-deferred over generations. Many 401(k) plans don't allow for this advantageous strategy.

How a Stretch IRA Works.*

Example: Papa John is 70 years old and is married to Jane, who is 66 years old. They have a 35-year-old daughter Jamie. John, the father, has accumulated $300,000 in his IRA. He begins his required minimum distributions when he reaches age 70 ½ based on his life expectancy of 13 years.

Beginning balance:	$300,000
Total RMD's before taxes:	$199,081
Total RMD's after taxes:	$143,338
Years of RMD payments:	13

Jane, his spouse, is his sole beneficiary. She inherits John's IRA when she is 79. She rolls the IRA balance into her own IRA. Jane names her daughter Jamie as the sole beneficiary. Jane takes her Required Minimum Distributions on her life expectancy of approximately 10 years.

IRA Jane inherited from John:	$326,331
Jane's total RMD's before taxes:	$205,864
Jane's total RMD's after taxes:	$148,222
Jane's total years of RMD's:	10

Jamie inherits her mother's IRA when she is 58. Instead of cashing out, she begins Required Minimum Distributions based on her life expectancy of approximately 25 years. Jamie designates her son, Jimmy, as her sole beneficiary.

IRA Jamie inherited from Jane:	$285,399
Jamie's total RMD's before taxes:	$537,137
Jamie's total RMD's after taxes:	$386,738
Jamie's total years of RMD's:	10

Jimmy inherits his mother Jamie's IRA and decides to cash it in to pay off his debts.

IRA Jimmy inherited from Jamie:	$121,128
Jimmy's total before taxes:	$121,128
Jimmy's total after taxes:	$87,212

Over three generations, John's $300,000 IRA paid his family over $1,063,209 before taxes! Unless this kind of opportunity for your family isn't important to you, you might want to make sure your retirement account is at a place where a Stretch IRA is possible.

If not, your family might just say, "He should have listened!"

**Note: This illustration assumes a 6% average annual total return and does not represent the performance of any specific investment. There is no guarantee of a 6% average annual return. The differences between actual and hypothetical results can result in significant differences between this illustration and the actual required distributions. The examples don't take into consideration estate taxes, but assumes a federal income tax rate of 28%. RMD's are calculated using life expectancy factors from the Uniform Lifetime Table for IRA owners and Single Life Expectancy Table for non-spouse beneficiaries (IRS Publication 590).*

Understanding Your 401(k) Options

Once you understand that your 401(k) plan may not be the best place to leave retirement money, it's important to know your options. First, you can stay put and enjoy the same portfolio of funds that you may have liked, the same tax-deferred growth, and litigation protection for up to a million dollars. Truly not a bad place to be.

Yet, you may very well "see the light" and decide to head for greener pastures. Many Plans have what is called an "In-Service, Non-Hardship Distribution" clause which allows you the availability of some, if not all, of your plan funds prior to retirement, post age 59 and a half. The IRS allows you to rollover your plan assets into a qualified IRA plan without taxation or a penalty so there is no reason for your employer's plan not to allow it. It is usually an oversight, if anything.

"Employers and 401(k) plan administrators don't advertise this fact, but most workers 59 and a half and older, and even some younger ones, ***can roll over 401(k) funds while they're still working...70% of companies--and 89% of those with 5,000 or more employees--allow these in-service withdrawals****, the Profit Sharing/401k Council of America found in a 2006 survey of 1,000 firms....* ***As for younger folks, the law permits them to get in-service distributions*** *of money rolled over from previous 401(k)s; of employer (but not*

employee) pretax contributions; of employee after-tax contributions; and of account earnings contributing to the plan..." (10)

There are many advantages of In-Service, Non-Hardship Distributions.

1. **Create Income Solutions.** As I mentioned in the previous chapter, you can create numerous plans for retirement income guaranteed using annuities that aren't available in most 401(k) plans. Remember when it comes to income, guarantees are extremely important. A "hope and a prayer" plan does not get it done. 401(k) plans offer little else by way of withdrawals.
2. **Diversity.** The options of the investment universe open up to you outside a 401(k) plan. This is especially true for the conservative investor seeking to put a portion of their retirement assets in protected vehicles. Remember the three Green Money Rules and they are available outside the 401(k) plan.
3. **Qualified Plan Consolidation.** If you are tired of getting statements from various IRA's, 401(k)'s, 403(b)'s or other plans representing the companies you worked with and want to consolidate them altogether under one roof it is available only outside your 401(k) plan. Isn't it true that as you get older you tend to forget more and long for simplicity.
4. **More Beneficiary Options.** Much like the lack of investment options for conservative investors, the 401(k) plan offers limited opportunities for serious estate planning.
5. **Availability of Stretch IRA.** No doubt about it, not using a Stretch IRA or Multi-Generational IRA format can cost your family millions. Don't miss this one.
6. **Get Some Professional Help if Desired.** There is also a universe of professionals available to you

> outside your 401(k) Plan. If you want to rid yourself of the disconnect between Wall Street and your retirement account, find a planner who understands the ABC's of Conservative Investing and get the protection you desire for the money you plan to live on the rest of your life.

Replacing your 401(k) with a rollover to a qualified IRA and choosing a professional that will guide you along the path to retirement security using conservative ABC strategies is a heck of a lot easier than a never-ending remodeling project.

In the end you'll be happy and won't be saying…"I should have listened."

- Twelve -

You Need a Sherpa: Choosing a Planner

A Mount Everest Mystery

Mt. Everest is 29,028 feet high. Let's just say it's a big mountain. Sir Edmund Hillary is reported to be the first one to scale the mountain.

"The expedition reached the South Peak on May, but all but two of the climbers who had come this far were forced to turn back by exhaustion at the high altitude. At last, Hillary and Tenzing Norgay, a native Nepalese climber who had participated in five previous Everest trips, were the only members of the party able to make the final assault on the summit. At 11:30 on the morning of May 29, 1953, Edmund Hillary and Tenzing Norgay reached the summit, 29,028 feet above sea level, the highest spot on earth. As remarkable as the feat of reaching the summit was the treacherous climb back down the peak." (1)

While Hillary is widely accepted as the first to summit Mt. Everest, two other men—George Mallory and Andrew Irvine—have been argued to have gotten there ahead of him 30 years earlier, yet it is still a mystery.

Noel Odell in his book "The Fight for Everest 1924" ponders whether Mallory and Irvine had reached the summit in 1924. He reports,

"The question remains, 'Has Mount Everest been climbed?' It must be left unanswered, for there is no direct evidence. But bearing in mind all the circumstances I have set out.... considering their position when last seen, I think to

myself there is a strong probability that Mallory and Irvine succeeded." (2)

The reason there is uncertainty is that the bodies of the two men were never found. Their campsite short of the summit was visited and left confusing evidence, along with Irvine's ice-pick just short of the summit. Noel Odell was the last to see them disappear into the clouds on a good pace for the summit. Yet, they never returned and their bodies never officially recovered. The historians are not sure if they summated and died on the way back or simply expired on the way to the top. It is a mountain climbing mystery and legend of sorts.

The question you might ask is why did Hillary succeed in making the climb and Mallory died? Among many possible reasons, including advances in climbing technology, is who they chose to climb with. Mallory chose to climb with his friend Andrew Irvine while Hillary selected an experienced mountain guide named Tenzing Norgay, a local Sherpa. Mallory chose a friend, Hillary chose a professional guide.

One of the benefits of finding a professional guide is they not only know the way up the mountain, but also know how to descend the mountain, which is reportedly more dangerous. Many climbers who summit the mountain have died on the way down. It would be incredibly valuable to have a professional guide who knows the terrain, the hidden hazards, and the safe paths.

When you consider where you are in climbing the retirement mountain, if you are reading this book, you are most likely either near the summit, at the summit, or heading down the mountain. You need a professional guide who knows the financial terrain, the hidden income hazards, and the safe investment paths. You need a financial Sherpa.

How do you find a Sherpa, a financial planner that fits what you need? Many in the financial industry and academia will give you a laundry list of questions, qualities, and designations that will make you feel very insecure. I believe there are three important characteristics to consider when looking for a planner: trust, like-ability, and competence.

Trust

Obviously one of the key characteristics, if not the most essential quality of a planner, is integrity. The planner must be someone you can trust not only with your most personal financial information, but detailed family matters that impact your finances. You must be able to trust their ability to remain confidential, not sharing your personal information with other clients or those outside their practice who might profit from your information.

You want to be able to trust their advice is given with your best interest in mind, without any possible consideration of their financial benefit in putting a plan together. Planners have many "tugs on their soul" and conflicts of interest that can pull them in an unethical direction. The industry can turn good men into people they don't want to be. Yet, there are those who have stayed the course and fought for the best interest of their clients. These are the men and women worth doing business with. No degree or designation is given for integrity. You have to find it by other means.

We know trust is something that is earned over time in a relationship. Unless you have missed something along the line, business is relational top to bottom. Trust in a relationship is earned when people do what they say they are going to do when they say they are going to do it. Trust is earned when planners anticipate the needs of a client and communicate on a regular basis. One of the sure keys to a trustworthy advisor is his method and amount of communication with his clients. Some use stale newsletters as the only way they communicate, or statements that seem to be written in Egyptian Hieroglyphics. How a planner communicates in a personal manner on an individual basis and what initiates that conversation is incredibly important.

A planner asked me not too long ago what I did to attract new business. I told him I rely on my relationships with my current clients to create new clients. I told him I believe my clients are out in their communities talking about their experiences. One of their experiences is the relationship with their financial planner. I told him they definitely talk about their relationship, good or bad. My clients, for the most part, are telling people about the positive nature of working with me and my office. It's through that relationship new clients come into my practice.

Incredibly, his response was, "I don't want a relationship. I want to sell them something."

As I said, trust is earned through a relationship. I think you and I know why this gentleman struggles to get new clients.

If trust is earned over time, how do you go about finding someone who can help get your initial ABC plan together? I suggest you "borrow" some trust. You probably have some friends who have a relationship with a planner. Ask them about their experience in working with their planner and if it sounds good to you, visit with the planner. You can "borrow" your friend's already developed trust, until you develop your own trust.

Another way to check on the credibility of an advisor is to ask the planner to let you call a couple of their current clients. Of course, they will give you only the clients they have a good relationship with, but that's fine. Call their clients and ask them to tell you about their "experience" of working with the planner. What is his style of communication? How do you feel when they are explaining investment options to you? Does he talk down to you or over your head? Do they communicate regularly?

Notice all these questions relate to the "experience" of working with a planner. We are trying to get a feel for how they trust their planner, not whether he's competent or not. You may want to ask them about the investments, but there are two things wrong with that question. First, you are now entering personal information territory. Most people don't want to reveal the types of assets and the performance of those assets, considering it is personal information. Second, most people don't understand the details and nuances of the investments they have. They could give you totally inaccurate information. This type of information you need to receive from the planner themselves.

Finally, you could attend a planner's workshop, if they conduct them, and get a feel for who they are as they relate with other people. Some planners may have great relationships with clients, but are somewhat uncomfortable up in front of a group, so this isn't the best way to determine the character of your potential planner. Yet, often a series of workshops conducted by a planner may give you the opportunity to check them out in a classroom style setting over a two- to three-session event.

All in all, trust is the key element of all business relationships. You will be able to develop it over time with a planner who has integrity, and there are ways to check it out at the beginning.

Like-ability

You might be thinking this may be the craziest way to determine the type of planner you want to work with, but think about it for just a minute. You will be working with this planner for years to come if you make a good choice. Do you really want to sit in an office with someone who irritates your socks off?

The question is, is he or she the "kind of person" you would want to work with? You really don't want to dread the communication from your planner. I know I'm going to hurt someone's feelings here, but if calling your financial planner for assistance is anything like calling your dentist for a root canal, you have the wrong guy (sorry, dentists).

How do you determine what the "kind of person" is the planner you would like to work with? First, you have to know a little about yourself. In doing so, I think Tim Templeton's description of four business temperaments in his book *The Referral of a Lifetime* (3) might be helpful. I'll attempt to describe them, though the labels are Tim's:

Relational/Relational: These are folks who start and end with the love of relationships. They are people-people inside and out. Somehow business just happens.

Relational/Business: R/B people have an easy time developing relationships, but when the topic turns to business, they quickly get in to tactical mode.

Business/Relational: B/R people may be a little uncomfortable with relationships upfront and use "business talk" as a way to get started. However, once people become their clients, the relationships are long and fulfilling. They have very loyal clients.

Business/Business: B/B people are those who are not relationally motivated on the front end or the back end of a business relationship. They are business all the time and somehow relationships happen. It's wrong to think that this is not the kind of person you would want simply because of the business nature of the advisor. There are people who need financial advice that are B/B also, and the R/R person irritates them to no end! (4)

The key is to identify what type you are and then find the planner who fits your mold. Be aware that you will typically be a good fit with 3 out of the 4 temperaments. As in most relationships, opposites sometimes attract, but it can end up in a "fatal attraction" with you not getting your needs met in the planning relationship. Most often it happens when a Relational/Relational gets together with the Business/Business temperament. "Danger Will Robinson! Danger!"

So, find the advisor who makes you feel comfortable and is a pleasure to be around. It's different and unique for everyone, but it matters just as much as being knowledgeable about finances.

Competence

Obviously, you want an advisor with competence in what they do. By competence, I mean they have acquired enough experience and knowledge to do the task you need done. You can investigate this again by asking for referrals and asking their clients about the advisor's competence. Visiting the advisor's workshops and client events are other ways of hearing them espouse their philosophy and financial planning techniques.

There are varying levels of financial planning in the industry. The Board of Certified Financial Planners considers three types of financial planning, all of which require different levels of information and training, yet all require the advisor to be diligent in his efforts and knowledgeable about the tasks.

The first is a single-issue plan. In other words, you need one facet of your finances dealt with in a competent manner, such as life insurance, or an annuity. You find a planner with an expertise in that asset and use them for your planning needs.

Second, you have a multi-strategy approach combining several types of assets in a financial plan. The plan may include Life Insurance, Health Insurance, and an annuity.

Lastly, you might need a comprehensive plan that involves everything you do financially. Life insurance, annuities, health insurance, property casualty insurance, tax planning, mutual funds, stocks, bonds, and even a revocable trust might be needed to accomplish your planning desires. For this, you would need an advisor who would quarterback a team of professionals.

The CFP Board considers all of these valid types of financial plans. Obviously, these three types of planning require varying degrees of competence. (5)

I believe that a planner cannot possibly be an expert on all financial matters. Rather, a planner has to become a specialist in a smaller segment of the market—focus their efforts on a niche market and pursue excellence by a course of study and experiences. How those courses of study and experiences evolve is different for each advisor. While some may pursue academic degrees and professional designations, others pursue a highly focused course of personal study, making use of the vast storehouses of materials and training events that occur at least monthly across the country. I believe the CFA, CFP, CLU, ChFC and other designations to be of great value, yet they are not the last word in competence.

In my practice, I have had the opportunity to train agents, brokers, attorneys, accountants, and others from around the country on the ever-changing fields of estate and financial planning. In so doing, I have learned from some of the best advisors in the country over the last fifteen years.

I have learned from men and women like Mike Dressander, Steve DeJohn, Tom Jackson(ChFC, CLU), Tom McNeily (ChFC), David and Katrina Savage, Chris Shreves and Navi Dowty who is a Chartered Financial Analyst (CFA) which is a large step above the vaunted CFP designation. Navi is an absolutely brilliant man with expertise and interests both in and out of the financial services industry of which he is a 39-year veteran.

Mike Dressander is a uniquely gifted entrepreneur who has developed one of the most prolific annuity Field Marketing Organizations in the country. I can tell you it is built not only on his vast knowledge of the annuity business, but on an overdeveloped sense of fairness.

Steve DeJohn, who is a graduate of Marquette University, has an incredible ability to explain the reasons index annuities have a place in any portfolio of assets, and he is one of the most loyal men I've ever known.

Tom Jackson finished two tours of Vietnam as a helicopter pilot. He's been shot at and shot down. I've seen the pictures. After he served his country faithfully and heroically, he became a CPA and financial advisor. With over 35 years of practice, Tom is one of the best out there at actually listening to a client and putting a plan together that proves itself over the years. His clients are extremely loyal.

Tom McNeily has a passion for protected money strategies and making sure his clients never lose a dime. He is a living testimony to me of passion and endurance in a constantly changing industry.

David and Katrina Savage work with churches, helping their people make sense out of a difficult investment world. Their common sense approach to investing and their unwavering integrity should be something advisors strive for.

Chris Shreves company motto is "because we care." The crazy thing is, he really does care about his clients, not just their money, but what goes on in their lives as well. You can't be around Chris for very long without realizing the passion he has for people.

Patrick Wehrly is truly one of the more unique and gifted, energetic and creative, financial planners I've come across.

Patrick brings a wide variety of life experience to his many years as a financial planner. He is an enrolled agent with the IRS, a real estate guru, a coast-guard rated Captain, and does missionary work in Central America, all while caring deeply about his clients.

These men and women have demonstrated that competence is developed by focusing on a segment of the market and concentrating on what it takes to solve the problems in that arena. They all do planning in the Boomer and Retiree market with excellence and integrity. There are many more that I don't have room to mention in this writing, but are equally capable, ethical and competent.

I tell you about these planners because they all demonstrate competence in their own way. If you want to find a competent planner, find one who's not trying to be everything to everybody. Find someone who's not trying to sell life insurance to 30-year-olds while making an income plan for a 62-year-old retiring couple.

Find someone who, like the famous football Coach Vince Lombardi, is chasing perfection and catching a little excellence along the way.

Questions You Might Ask a Potential Advisor:

- What is your area of specialty? Do you have an area of focus?
- What is your investment philosophy?
- How long have you been a planner?
- If you haven't been in the business long, who do you have as a mentor or back-up planner to help you plan?
- What licenses do you hold? Why those licenses?
- Do you have a planning team that includes attorneys or accountants or other advisors?
- Can I speak with 3-4 of your clients?
- Are you familiar with the ABC Model of Investing and do you use it in your planning?
- How do you make use of Fixed Index Annuities in your practice?

- Do you consider yourself a "safe money specialist?"
- Tell me about the manner in which you communicate with your clients.
    - Do you have client events?
    - Do you have a newsletter?
- Do you conduct regular reviews with your clients, and if so, how often?
- If I have a question after I become a client of yours, whom do I speak with?
- What types of assets do you use in planning?
- Can I visit your next client event?
- Are there any fees in working with you?
- Tell me about the planning process.
- Have you ever had any regulatory actions taken against you?

These are not an exhaustive list of questions, but it will definitely get you on the right road.

Becoming a Client-Partner

First, I want to say that as a planner, I hate asking for referrals. It's uncomfortable for me and for my clients. I think its imposing on them. Advisors have used the same tired old tactics to ask for referrals forever. It is distasteful. I just don't believe in it.

Something I do believe in is a partnership between the client and advisor. The advisor's role is to create, implement, and adjust the financial plan tailored to the needs of the client. The advisor is partnering with the client to see them succeed in their retirement. Partnership is a two-way street by definition. The role of this client partnership is very important.

The role of the Client-Partner is to talk with others about the experience of working with the advisor and invite them to meet the advisor at a client event, workshop, or at an individual conference. As you are out in the community with your friends, family, and acquaintances, the subject of finances comes up. All you need to do is say, "you might want to speak with my advisor Dave." If they say they already have an advisor, drop the subject. Yet, if they ask you who your advisor is, tell them about the "experience" of working with him. Then simply invite them to meet with you and your advisor for lunch (the advisor will pay), or invite them to the next client event or workshop. This will enable your friend to meet your advisor in a casual setting to see if your advisor is the "kind of person" they might want to work with.

You can always call your advisor after speaking with your friend and get permission to have them call your friend. The advisor can take it from there.

The relationship of an advisor and client-partner can be a long and prosperous one for both parties. Bringing your friends who've expressed a financial need to meet your advisor is a major compliment. Finding an advisor you trust, like, and is competent makes it all the more enjoyable.

It is obvious that you need a financial Sherpa to help you summit the retirement mountain and descend in a safe manner. Finding that advisor shouldn't be a mystery.

- Thirteen -

Deal or No Deal: Process, Process, Process

Game Show Stress

Game shows are really a hoot to watch, aren't they? I know you probably have your favorite show, but one of my all time favorites is "Deal or No Deal" with Howie Mandel. People are absolutely hysterical on that show. Honestly, where do they find them?

The contestant is charged with the task of picking briefcases one by one, trying to eliminate all but the Million Dollar briefcase which he hopes is on a table at his side. There are thirty beautiful models standing on a layer of steps smilingly tempting the contestant to choose their case. Then there's the man upstairs who phones in a bid to try and stop the contestant from winning a bigger pot. The contestant has to decide on the offer, "Deal or No Deal." The contestant chooses to accept the offer or continue to eliminate the briefcases filled with amounts ranging from $1 to $1,000,000, hoping the million is in the case on the table.

His family and friends are there giving advice to Deal or No Deal. The audience is shouting and Howie is "counseling" them through the process. It is incredible the amount of people who will give up a $200,000 producer's offer and end up getting $50 all in the pursuit of a million dollars. The show runs on the ramped up emotion of pure greed. They want that million dollars and they sing, dance, jump, sweat laugh, cry, and...I'm wiped out just thinking about it.

Is that any way to make a financial decision? Of course not!

Three Elements of a Financial Decision

Once you have found an advisor (hopefully not Howie) you will have some decisions to make regarding the plans and assets they propose for your finances. It might be helpful to know how people typically work through a decision and what a planning process should look like. Knowing this will help you work through your personal decision-making agenda. It will also assist you in seeing how a good planning process helps make confident decisions that affect the rest of your lives in retirement.

It's a very interesting study when we look into the factors that affect our decision making. I believe there are three aspects of making decisions regarding financial planning: logic, emotion, and beliefs. (1)

Logic

First, is the area of logic—the science of reasoning. In other words, it's how we "make sense" of something. We have an innate need to reasonably work through an issue with facts and details. We need to rationally decide on an issue.

One of the problems Wall Street has is its inability to be rational. The Wall Street mentality, "greed is good" is a prime example. The Wall Street retirement philosophy has been advertised with life lived on a five-star golf course, vacations all over the world, hot cars, expensive jewelry, and a mystical green path directing you to your own personal pot of gold. Wall Street says you have a "number" and your "number" takes a beating in a nasty world, but they can magically protect your "number" with mutual fund pixie dust.

If you buy into the media fantasies of Wall Street greed, then you will spend your retirement chasing after money and making the materialistic goal of outgaining your neighbors your priority. In the end, much like Wall Street you are chasing the wind and you will always have a deeply seeded feeling of anxiety and frustration with your results. Who can catch the wind? You? Someone will always have more than you do, their funds will gain more than yours, and they will have more "stuff." You can spend an entire lifetime chasing the wind only to find out it can't be caught. Greed is not good.

As John, my trainer says, "There's a disconnect between Wall Street and reality." Now John's a physical trainer at a health club, and if he can see it, I imagine you can too. If John's right, then veering away from the Wall Street media images and logically, reasonably, and rationally pursuing your financial goals brings fulfillment in the end. You need to see how a plan works "realistically" and not with a greedy goal. That's why ABC Investing is so important. You need to have real guarantees where they are needed, especially when it comes to income planning. Not a false promise of "safety" while being exposed to credit risk.

You need to be able to look at your plan and say to yourself, "Now, that makes sense!"

Beliefs

Secondly, beliefs can be the stimulus for either a good or bad buying decision. What you believe about a topic will eventually determine how you feel about it. Counselors spend hours and hours trying to discover the beliefs of their patients driving their behaviors. For instance, if you have an underlying belief that money is evil, you will continually battle the idea of making more of it. If you believe money is king, then you won't be satisfied until you've tried every avenue leaving no stone unturned, including shady investment schemes, to try and get rich. Beliefs matter.

I have often told my son, "...emotions will eventually follow what you believe to be true, so *find out what the truth is and believe that...*your emotions will catch up eventually." Our emotions follow what we believe. We tend to get it backwards and follow our emotions far too much, so beliefs are crucial.

Wall Street tries its best to instill a belief system that is disconnected from reality at its best. If you believe that brokers are in the business only to make money at the expense of their clients, then you will have trouble listening to and following professional advice. If you believe only "irrational" people would buy an index annuity, then you will run the other way missing out on the guarantees. If you believe large wire houses are the only place to get professional advice, then you will miss out on some incredibly talented professionals, while buying into the greed is good mentality.

Worse yet, if your beliefs are fictional beliefs, you will invest in "wonderland" with Alice and watch your money go down the rabbit's hole with Johnny Depp, I mean the Mad Hatter, as your broker. Think I'm wrong?

A fictional belief is something we believe in that just isn't true. We acquired the belief through the media, friends, neighbors, brokers or other venues that we trust, yet the information is incorrect or the conclusions are skewed. We compile these beliefs over time and they dramatically affect the decisions we make.

One of the realities that every investor has to deal with is "bias," which is a belief which prevents an unprejudiced consideration of a position. Bias is a distorted view that prevents impartiality. (2) Everyone has a bias. I have a bias. I am a conservative advisor whose career started in the insurance industry and added securities, or risk products, along the way. Authors who write articles for financial magazines, or analysts on financial television and radio shows, all have a background that lends itself to bias. No one is free of it.

As you listen to someone with a background in the securities industry demean an insurance product like an index annuity you have to realize his or her conclusions are fraught with bias. If you hear a radio program by an insurance agent who trashes brokers and the security industry, obviously he's biased. The consumer is inundated with these influences on a global basis. You can't escape it. The information you are receiving is tainted and you are forming beliefs, siding with a bias.

Your job is to "find out the truth and deal with that." What is truth? (Now there's an age-old question.) The truth deals with realism and facts. You have to be open to the reality that what you believe may in fact come from a bias, which can prevent you from making the most beneficial of plans. This is especially true in conservative investing. There are planners whose bias lends them to the belief every financial goal can be accomplished through the use of securities like stocks, bonds, mutual funds, derivatives, etc. This is simply not true. Not for the conservative investor whose emotions can't take much fluctuation in their accounts or some who can't take any uncertainty in their accounts. They never want to see a loss. Ever! Yet, Wall Street keeps coming at them with a plan totally disconnected to their desires. That's the belief system of Wall Street. These are not the beliefs of a conservative investor.

On the other hand, there are agents in the insurance industry that believe securities are too risky for retirees and index annuities are the only answer. They too are wrong. Even though a conservative investor may not want market risk, it doesn't mean all their money should be placed in annuities.

Challenge your beliefs. You have had a mental intravenous feeding of Wall Street's philosophy day in and day out. Challenge it. A conservative investor has to fly in the face of Wall Street beliefs. That's why the ABC Model helps a conservative investor determine how much risk to allow into their portfolio. An agent or broker who understands the ABC Model can help you sift through your beliefs.

Find out what the truth is and believe that.

Emotions

While beliefs can lead our emotions, the third facet of making a decision is firmly planted in that elusive realm. We all like to believe when we make a purchasing decision we have made it on a completely rational basis. Yet, every study in academia shows buying is an emotional decision. Make no mistake about it. When you are planning your retirement and choosing conservative methods and financial tools, your emotions are fully engaged.

In fact, there are whole divisions within universities that study the emotional dynamics of investing labeled "behavioral finance," along with the impact of emotions on economies.

John W. Rogers, Jr. emphasizes the point in his column "The Patient Investor" on Forbes.com:

> *"...behavioral academics are on the firmest ground citing the madness-of-crowds phenomenon. Most people make the same mistakes over and over. The most prevalent one is to pile in at the peak with everyone else. Since fitting in is easier than sticking out, investors flock together even when the results turn out bad." (3)*

In a typical Boom/Bust market cycle people are most often joining a "Buying Spree" near the top of the Bull market when enthusiasm is high. Then investors typically participate in a "Selling Spree" near the bottom of the market in a panic. This "madness-of-crowds phenomenon" runs in contrast to the age-old "buy low, sell high" axiom which instructs us to make the most out of the market by buying when it is at the bottom and selling out when you have made money. Remember, Baron Rothschild's advice on when to buy is when there is "blood in the streets." (4)

It's clear to me that conservative investors need to understand their emotional involvement when buying and selling assets. One of the keys to work through emotions is simply to be aware of them. If you know you are feeling invincible, you want to be careful about investing. As is true for when you are having a panic attack regarding the market. If you are looking to invest, because everyone you know is kicking butt in the market, don't. You will probably end up with a sore back side when the market kicks your butt in the freefall.

As I have stated earlier, your emotions are valid when determining how much risk you want in your portfolio. Risk is how you "feel" about uncertainty in the market. Using a risk tolerance questionnaire can facilitate a more objective evaluation of how much risk you want in a portfolio. You don't need a questionnaire to find out if you are conservative. You already know that. What you need to work through emotions when investing is a sound planning process.

Process, Process, Process

In battling emotional investing, you need a process to work through to protect yourself from making a potentially devastating purchasing decision. I suggest a process of investigation, recommendation, and implementation, followed by a healthy dose of review and adjustments. This process should help you work through your emotions, challenge your beliefs, and reasonably pursue a financial decision. The process should give you the time to make an informed decision.

Different planners plan differently. You can set your own pace in a decision making process by establishing the ground rules at the beginning of your work with an advisor. Knowing a simple planning system you can use with advisors will be helpful.

The first planning step is "investigation." During this step, you will discover all the risk, leaks, and gaps in your current financial plan. You should fill out a financial review form listing all your assets (appendix chapter one) and income. The financial review form can help you see your assets as a whole and how they relate to each other. You will want to list the concerns you have about your assets, your goals, and of course decide on the ABC Allocation you believe best fits you. You will want to pay close attention to the time horizon you have for your goals. This is crucial when it comes to deciding on the assets you use in your plan. An advisor can help you think through possible solutions to the concerns and goals you have.

Second, either develop for yourself or receive from an advisor a plan which includes everything your goals set out to accomplish. This plan should be detailed and involve assets and income from specific sources. The plan should include what you want to accomplish in at least the next five years with an ability to adjust as necessary.

Third, implement your plan when you have worked out the details and you are confident it is a solution to problems—one that will accomplish your goals. It will involve a lot of paperwork and is best done in a separate meeting so you have time to go over the details with your advisor. You will most likely have to make transfers into different companies, which will create a conservation attempt in some form, by the current company holding your money. Just remember, it's your money, not theirs. This is something they often forget.

Lastly, you will want to review the plan once all the monies are transferred to make sure they are where you wanted them to be and in the amounts you had determined for your plan. I would suggest you review the plan at least every six months to make sure you are on the right path. If you have assets in Column C, the Red Risk portion, you will want some type of a review quarterly. Remember your goals and especially your time horizon. For conservative investors this is not a sprint, but a marathon. Patience is required for life in the slow lane.

I know at times working through your retirement goals has been a lot like a game show. Yet, unlike Deal or No Deal, you have a choice to work through a process in which you could actually realize your goals for retirement using a conservative approach to planning. Given the right process, your emotions will be given the opportunity to be led by your beliefs, which will be challenged by the truth, leading to a logical conclusion.

Or you could just scream and yell and pick and choose and laugh and cry and…oh, you've already done that. Well then, let's try something new. Let's try a planning process not a game show to accomplish your goals.

Deal or No Deal?

- Fourteen -

Seven Steps to an ABC Plan

Review

Hopefully you have been having a little fun along these pages listening to my stories and opinions. I also hope if you have connected emotionally with the idea that Wall Street is disconnected with Main Street, you are ready to "re-connect" with reality, take some action and get your ABC Plan together.

The ABC Model of Investing is meant to simplify the process for those conservative, Main Street investors who are tired of having too much uncertainty in their portfolio.

Reading through these pages, you have learned conservative investing is not a fad. It's not investing in the mutual fund flavor of the month. It's not Vegas either. Yet the "Vegas Mentality" has had a dramatic impact on the way Americans invest. Conservative investing is long-haul, throw excess risk out the window investing. It's life in the slow lane.

Conservative investors are those who cringe at the mere thought of risk in their portfolio. They may take a small amount of it, but very small. They don't buy into the Wall Street myths wire house brokers have been feeding us for years. They actually believe their account statement when it says they have either gained or lost over the last quarter. They think "buy & hold" is dead and just sitting on an index fund for ten years could lose them another 20%. They believe scattering all of your assets over asset classes doesn't prevent market losses, and index annuities are not great white sharks, but just possibly lifeboats to a sinking industry.

Conservative investors believe large shifts in the economy and in investing happen without warning, and there are no crystal balls to see the future. Conservative investors want to have certainty in uncertain times. They want protection and guarantees on the largest portion of their assets and tactical management on the smaller risk portion of their portfolio.

You discovered the ABC model of investing and its simplicity. Putting money proportionally in three categories that match your time horizon and risk tolerance is probably something you could think through easily enough. Yellow Money is your short-term cash reserves. Green Money follows three rules: protect your principal, retain your gains, and guarantee your income. Red Money is the only place for market risk in your portfolio, using two types of risk: stock-type risk and bond-type risk.

You have also learned that using the ABC Model of Investing can help prevent a lost decade similar to 2000 through 2009, by relying heavily on the Green Money column to provide protected money gains, along with tactical management of Red Risk money. Conservative investors are not unlike other Americans retiring with their greatest need being an income which lasts longer than ever before in retirement history. Rolling over your 401(k) plan is probably the doorway to the larger universe of investment options and income plans.

I think you, probably like most retiring Americans, see the need for a complete estate plan that you can mold throughout your retirement years. Finding an advisor who can quarterback an estate planning team may be what you need to find, or maybe you just need a few small adjustments in an already created plan, with some larger adjustments to your portfolio. Whichever is the case, you could use some help in investigating a plan specifically tailored to your needs. You could use an advisor who understands that a process helps you through the emotional struggles of developing your plan.

Here we are at the end, and you probably need just a little help in getting started. A list maybe, which could outline the steps you could take to making your own ABC Plan.

Funny you should ask. I just happen to have a list.

7 Steps to an ABC Plan

Step One: Get Your Assets Together

Begin by gathering your most recent asset statements. The following is a partial list of statements to gather:

- ✓ Brokerage accounts
- ✓ Mutual funds
- ✓ IRA, 401(k), 403(b) and other qualified plans
- ✓ Annuities
- ✓ Bank accounts, including CD's, savings, and money market accounts
- ✓ Stock certificates
- ✓ Bonds, including government savings bonds
- ✓ Life Insurance
- ✓ Precious Metals
- ✓ Real Estate

Take the statements to your advisor and they will gladly make you copies. Use one of the Asset Review Forms in Appendix One to assist you in arranging your finances so you can see the "big picture." Getting all your assets together and making a list benefits you in many ways. If something were to happen to you, your spouse or heirs would have a current list of assets. It also helps your think more clearly about your finances rather than having a scattered idea of what you own.

Step Two: Write It Down

Using the forms in Appendixes One and Two to write down your thoughts will help organize your thinking before seeing an advisor. You will want to write down the greatest concerns you have about your assets and your goals for the near and far future.

Write down some of the things that worry you most about your financial situation. If you can't think of any big worries, then remember everyone has a "pebble in the shoe." In other words, something which may be small, but it irritates the heck out you. If you have ever had a pebble in your shoe when walking or running a long distance and ended up with a huge blister or sore on your foot, you know exactly what I'm talking about. If you have a pebble in the shoe financially, now is the time to deal with it. It may be a certain asset like a bond, or mutual fund you've had a long time and isn't a lot of money, but it has frustrated you the whole time you have had it.

Your frustrations and fears can also be large enough to keep you awake at night. Maybe you are struggling to gain enough assets to retire on, or your income is changing soon and you're not sure how to replace it. Your current advisor might not communicate with you, or you are just worried about the path the economy is on and want off the roller coaster. All of these are valid and need to be expressed on the list.

Written goals are a sure way to guarantee you will be able to know if you are on track with your investments. You will want to write down immediate goals, 1 year, 3 year, 5 year and even longer goals. You can always adjust your goals, but if you don't have anything to adjust, you end up lost. Remember, if you don't have a target to shoot at, you'll end up hitting anything.

Step Three: ABC Your Assets

Now you are ready to choose which types of assets you would want to invest in going forward. Pretend every asset is moveable and changeable, and then ask yourself if you could make a new plan starting today, what would that plan look like? You will want to distinguish your investible assets from your non-liquid assets. For instance, you might have invested in a rental home, which isn't a liquid asset, as opposed to a stock or mutual fund. Be sure and get a total of "investible assets" before trying to ABC them.

Remember there are three categories of assets Yellow, Green, and Red. What percent of your assets do you need in cash for emergencies, coming events, and if your income dries up for six months to a year? This is Yellow Column A money. Next, what percent do you want in the market with either bond-type risk or stock-type risk? This is Red Column C money.

Finally, add the two percentages you just wrote down and subtract it from 100, and this is the amount of money you want in the Green Column B. Keep in mind, the three Green Money rules which reduce market risk in your portfolio. Make use of the last page of the Financial Review Form in Appendix One.

Step Four: Choose an Advisor

Here is where the rubber meets the road. Deciding to take this step of finding an advisor means you are serious about your planning needs and want a conservative advisor. Go back to chapter 13 and figure out which temperament you are, then begin asking your friends about their advisors or visit a few seminars and workshops. Get a feel for who is out there in your market place.

Next, look over the questions to ask an advisor in Chapter 12 and take them with you to interview your prospective agent. You might very well be in a class going over this material and the advisor you've spent time with seems to your liking. Run through the questions with them. Once you are satisfied that they understand conservative investing and they have demonstrated a competence, go ahead to Step Five.

Just a thought. Whether your advisor is an insurance agent or a securities broker, or both, doesn't matter. You want someone who understands the ABC's of Conservative Investing and is able to facilitate that style of plan for your benefit. There are many, many different types of financial licenses and designations, but in the long run, they need to understand you, how you want to invest conservatively, and do it competently.

Step Five: Process, Process, Process

Now is the time to work through a planning process with the advisor. If he is trained in the ABC's, then he or she is familiar with the steps of Investigate, Recommend, Implement, Review and Adjust. These steps will help you challenge your fictional beliefs, and work through your emotions while travelling down a logical path to financial success.

I find the plan will come with two facets: overview and detail. You will want to understand the "big picture" of your plan while also digging into details. What's that saying, "it's the little things that matter?" I agree.

Step Six: Review & Adjust

Once you have implemented your plan with the advisor, decide on a schedule of reviews that meets your needs best. Get on their calendar right away, as it will give you confidence knowing you have the opportunity to review the plan again and see if it is going according to the projections and parameters you originally laid out.

It's also in this step that you take the initiative of a "client-partner." If you have had a good experience with your advisor, then "talk him up" to your family and friends. Ask your advisor for his calendar of client events so you can become part of the group and bring your friends who have expressed an interest in the advisor's services. I don't know why, but my clients love to come to the parties we have and bring their friends. They are constantly asking me when the next event is. I hope your experience is the same.

Step Seven: Sleep Easy

Finally! You thought this moment might never come. You've been so burned by brokers and Wall Street craziness that you honestly believed you would have to put up with it for the rest of your lives; and now you know it's not true. You can actually enjoy a good night's rest knowing that your ABC Plan has just the right amount of risk in it that only you can handle. It's your plan, not a Wall Street broker's plan.

In the end, conservative investing isn't anything like Batman socks or other fads. It is not the flavor of the month style of investing that has caught so many investors by surprise in a down market. Conservative investing is long-haul, core investing with just the right amount of risk tailored to your temperament.

My hope is that you have indeed resonated with the concepts involved in the ABC's of Conservative Investing and are willing to begin your seven steps to a peaceful night's rest.

Appendices

- Appendix One -

Financial Review Forms

On the following pages are two forms, the "Issues and Goals Review Form" and the "Financial Planning Data Form." The Issues and Goals form can be used to sort out your feelings surrounding the issues in financial planning and the goals you want to accomplish. These forms will help you accomplish steps two and three of "The ABC Plan in Seven Steps" outlined in Chapter 14.

The Financial Planning Data Form on the following pages will assist you in logging information needed to create your financial plan. It will also assist your ABC Financial Planner in understanding how you view of your assets.

Just take your time as you answer the questions; discuss them with your spouse, significant other, close friend, or financial advisor if possible. One of the best things you could do is to fill it out two different times, sharpening your thoughts each time.

Issues & Goals Review Form

What's Important to You?

(These are questions to help you discover your highest value needs.)

What were you hoping to accomplish
by making a financial plan?

What is important to you about:

1. Taxes
2. Safety
3. Guarantees
4. Long-Term Care Planning
5. Achieving Security
6. Income
7. Liquidity
8. Return on Investments
9. Diversification
10. Inflation
11. Passing Assets on to Heirs
12. Communication with your Agent/Broker

Highest Relational Needs & Expectations

What's Important to You?

(These are questions to help you discover your "rules for change.")

1. Of all the concerns listed above, how would you prioritize the importance of what you want to work on?

    a. What do you like or dislike about your current financial plan?

    b. How would you define success in your financial plan?

    c. What would you change?

    d. How do you determine "next steps"?

    e. What is your past experience with planners?

    f. What will be the response of your current advisor if you make changes with a different advisor?

    g. How would you respond?

    h. Who do you include when making decisions of this nature?

2. If you haven't solved these issues to date, why is it important that you take action now?

3. What are the most important things to you when it comes to partnering with a professional advisor?

4. If you could wave a magic wand and solve these issues, what would it look like?

Short- & Long-Term Goals

(These questions will help you think through your immediate, short-term and long-term goals.)

1. Do you live off the interest income of your investments?
    a. What is the amount of income derived from your assets?

2. Are you satisfied with your current income?
    a. If "No," explain.

3. Do you anticipate any changes in your annual income?
    a. If "Yes," explain.

4. Are you planning any major lifestyle changes?
    a. If "Yes," explain.

5. Do you see any large purchases in the next 2 to 5 years?
    a. If "Yes," explain.

6. Rate the importance of the items below from 1(most) to 5(least).
    a. Pay less income tax:___
    b. Reduce or eliminate estate tax:___
    c. Reduce or eliminate capital gains tax:___
    d. Increase monthly income:___
    e. Finding a good money manager for assets in the market:___
    f. Ensure that my assets are protected from market losses:___
    g. Increase my returns on savings and retirement funds:___
    h. Protection of principal:___
7. What do you want to accomplish with your assets over the next two years?

8. List three financial goals for the next three to five years.

9. List two financial goals for ten years from now.

10. List two financial goals beyond ten years.

Financial Planning Data Form

Family Information

Person #1: ________________________ Age:___ **M D W NM**
(Key: **M**arried/**D**ivorced/**W**idowed/**N**ot **M**arried)

SS#: ____-___-____ DOB: ___/___/___ Citizen of U.S. __ Yes __No

Person #2: ________________________ Age:___ **M D W NM**
(Key: **M**arried/**D**ivorced/**W**idowed/**N**ot **M**arried)

SS#: ____-___-____ DOB: ___/___/___ Citizen of U.S. __ Yes __No

Address: _____________________________ County: _____________

City: ______________________________ State: ___ Zip: ________

Home Phone: ____-____-______ Work Phone: _____-____-______

Children:___
Name:_____________________ Age:______ **M D W NM**
City/St:_____________________
Name:_____________________ Age:______ **M D W NM**
City/St:_____________________
Name:_____________________ Age:______ **M D W NM**
City/St:_____________________
Name:_____________________ Age:______ **M D W NM**
City/St:_____________________
Name:_____________________ Age:______ **M D W NM**
City/St:_____________________
Name:_____________________ Age:______ **M D W NM**
City/St:_____________________
Retirement Date(s):
Person #1:_________________ Person #2:___________________

Do you have a will? **Yes No** Do you have a trust? **Yes No**
Type of trust:____
Do you have a Property & Financial POA? **Yes No**
Do you have a Health Care POA? **Yes No** Living Will? **Yes No**
Disability: **Yes No**
Notes:

Financial Information

ASSETS	Cost Basis	Present Value	
Real Estate			Mortgage? Equity Loan?
Home	________	________	______________
Other Real Estate	________	________	______________
	________	________	______________
	________	________	______________
Cash			
Stocks	________	________	
Bonds	________	________	
Mutual Funds	________	________	
Business Interests	________	________	
Other Investments	________	________	
CDs & Savings Accts.	________		
Checking Accts.	________		
Personal Property			
Home Furnishings, Jewelry, Silverware, Antiques, & Collectibles	________		
Sub-Total - A	__________		

Primary Financial Objective
(Rank in order of importance):

____ Tax Deferral
____ Income Now
____ Growth
____ Estate Planning
____ Preservation of Principal
____ Other ____________

Willingness to Accept Risk for Additional Financial Performance (Choose One):

____ Aggressive
____ Moderate
____ Conservative

IRA's & Insurance

Husband's IRA	________
Wife's IRA	________
Pension (401, etc.)	________
Life Insurance	
Face Value/Cash Value	
________/________	
________/________	
________/________	

Annuities	Fixed	FIA	VA
________	___	___	___
________	___	___	___
________	___	___	___

Sub-Total - B __________
TOTAL – A+B __________

Income

__________ Husband's SS
__________ Wife's SS
__________ Pension
__________ Pension
__________ W2/1099
__________ W2/1099
__________ Other
__________ **Total**

Estimated Federal Tax Bracket:

___ 0-15%
___ 16-28%
___ 29-35%
___ 36% & up

Your ABC Profile

A	B	C	Comments
Cash Potentially Lower Returns Liquid & Taxable	**Protected Growth** Potentially Moderate Returns Offers Partial Withdrawals & Tax Deferral	**Risk Growth** Potentially Higher Returns Liquid & Taxable Stock Type Risk Bond Type Risk	
Preferred Percent in This Category	Preferred Percent in This Category	Preferred Percent in This Category	
Estimated Percent Already in This Category	Estimated Percent Already in This Category	Estimated Percent Already in This Category	

- Appendix Two -

Retirement Budget Worksheet

On the following pages you will find a sample retirement budget worksheet. Fill this form out when you are planning to retire in order to determine how much income you'll need in retirement. The form can also be used before retirement to anticipate the effects of major lifestyle changes such as a change in occupation or the death of a spouse.

Simply fill in the first column according to your current income and expenses. The second column is what you anticipate to spend. Subtract the second column from the first column and you will be able to determine what you will need for income when you retire.

Retirement Budget Worksheet

Expenses			
Item	**Current Budget**	**Retirement Budget**	**Difference**
Residence			
Rent or mortgage			
Real estate taxes			
Home Owners/Renters Insurance			
Furniture and furnishings			
Appliances			
Cleaning, repairs and maintenance			
Electricity, gas and heating			
Water and sewer			
Telephone, cell phone, cable			
Other			
Total Residence			

Retirement Budget Worksheet – Cont'd

Meals & Groceries			
Groceries & meals at home			
Meals outside the home			
Total Meals & Groceries			
Clothing			
Clothing, shoes, jackets, etc.			
Dry cleaning, laundry			
Jewelry.			
Total Clothing			
Personal			
Personal care and toiletries			
Child care			
Legal and accounting			
Life and disability insurance			
Other			
Total personal			
Transportation			
Vehicle payments			
Repairs and maintenance			
Insurance			
Gas, oil and tires			
Public transportation			
Other			
Total Transportation			
Healthcare			
Prescriptions			
Doctors, dentists and hospitals			
Health insurance			
Other			
Total Healthcare			
Debt, Savings and Investment			
Credit cards & other loans			
Investment dollars			
Emergency fund			
Vacation & entertainment savings			
Debt contraction			
Other			
Total Debt, Savings & Investments			

Retirement Budget Worksheet – Cont'd

Miscellaneous			
Books & other publications			
Vacations			
Entertainment and affiliations			
Charitable giving			
Education			
Investment costs			
Other			
Total Miscellaneous			
Total Expenses			

Income			
Item	**Current Budget**	**Retirement Budget**	**Difference**
Salary & Wages			
1099 Income			
Rental Income			
Dividends			
Interest			
Sale of assets			
Social Security			
Pensions			
Other			
Total Income			

	Current Budget	**Retirement Budget**	**Difference**
Net Income & Expenses			

- Appendix Three -

Risk Assessment Questionnaire

The following is a Risk Assessment Questionnaire used in the ABC's of Conservative Investing Workshop. It is provided courtesy of Dan Hunt and Redhawk Wealth Advisors, Inc. Simply follow the instructions and you will easily determine your risk tolerance. Remember, the questionnaire helps you determine the degree of your "upset-ness" when your investments don't perform as you expected they would.

Risk Tolerance Questionnaire

Please place the score on the line to the right by writing the number on the line.

1. **What is the time horizon (prior to income or systematic withdrawals) for this investment account?**
   (*EXAMPLE: answer a. would be a score of 0 on the line.)*

a.	Less than 3 years	____a.	0
b.	3 to 5 years	____b.	5
c.	5 to 10 years	____c.	7
d.	10 to 15 years	____d.	10
e.	Greater than 15 years	____e.	15

2. **What percentage of your liquid net worth is in principal protected products (i.e., Fixed Annuities, CDs, Life Insurance)?**

a.	Less than 10%	____a.	3
b.	Between 10% and 25%	____b.	5
c.	Between 25% and 50%	____c.	7
d.	Between 50% and 75%	____d.	10
e.	Greater than 75%	____d.	15

3. Investments that provide greater returns over the long run often are more volatile over the short run. Choose the answer that best describes your concerns about value changes:

a) Day-to-day fluctuations in the value of my investments make me very uncomfortable.

a. Strongly Agree	____a.	1
b. Agree	____b.	2
c. Neutral	____c.	3
d. Disagree	____d.	4
e. Strongly Disagree	____e.	5

b) Short-term volatility is acceptable when prospects of greater long-term gains exist.

a. Strongly Agree	____a.	5
b. Agree	____b.	4
c. Neutral	____c.	3
d. Disagree	____d.	2
e. Strongly Disagree	____e.	1

4. In the first year, if these assets lose 1/3 of their total value, but evidence suggests that the portfolio should probably recover enough to still meet your goal, how would you react?

a) Short-term losses are unacceptable even if historical evidence suggests my long-term goal is still achievable

a. Strongly Agree	____a.	1
b. Agree	____b.	2
c. Neutral	____c.	3
d. Disagree	____d.	4
e. Strongly Disagree	____e.	5

b) Short-term losses don't bother me as long as my long-term investment goal is still attainable.

a. Strongly Agree	____a.	5
b. Agree	____b.	4
c. Neutral	____c.	3
d. Disagree	____d.	2
e. Strongly Disagree	____e.	1

5. Expected Return. Use Chart to determine which risk best fits you?

____a. 1
____b. 3
____c. 5
____d. 7
____e. 10

Expected Average Return and Volatility (75% Probability) Expected Return:

a. Volatility between -3% to 15%, expected return of 6%
b. Volatility between -4% to 18%, expected return of 7%
c. Volatility between -6% to 22%, expected return of 8%
d. Volatility between -10% to 30%, expected return of 10%
e. Volatility between -14% to 36%, expected return of 12%

6. **Choose the statement that best reflects your thoughts about reaching your financial goals:**
I'm interested in stable growth in the value of my portfolio, even if it means accepting lower results in the long run.

a.	Strongly Agree	____a.	1
b.	Agree	____b.	3
c.	Neutral	____c.	5
d.	Disagree	____d.	7
e.	Strongly Disagree	____e.	10

7. **This investment represents approximately what percentage of your total investments, excluding your principal residence or vacation homes?**

a.	Greater than 75%	____a.	1
b.	Between 51% and 75%	____b.	2
c.	Between 25% and 50%	____c.	3
d.	Between 10% and 25%	____d.	4
e.	Less than 10%	____e.	5

Your total score will help us determine the appropriate investment profile (below): ________ Total Score

Total Score	**Risk Profile**
0 – 31	**Conservative**
32 – 63	**Moderate**
64 – 75	**Aggressive**

*Used by permission of Dan Hunt and Redhawk Wealth Advisors, Inc. 9/2010

- Appendix Four -

Red Risk Money Resources

I appreciate so many advisors around the country who have opted to use a "fee-based" platform and become a "fiduciary" in the process. These, I believe, are in the best interest of the client. The reasons are easily understood.

First, "fee-based" means the advisor is charging you based on your assets they manage. For instance, if you have a portfolio of $100,000, he may asses a 2% fee on those assets he actually manages. The fee would typically be assessed on a quarterly basis. Using this model as a base eliminates the use of commission-driven assets such as A-share, B-share, or C-share mutual funds. Typically the advisor will use a no-load, low expense fund in the investing model, or ETF. The fee-based advisor has a very real interest in your accounts doing well. If your accounts increase in value, they make more income. If your accounts decrease in value, they lose income. They are highly motivated!

Second, a "fiduciary" is expected to act in the best interests of the client, not the best interest of the advisor. That's why there is a limited use of commission-based assets. While planners still use Index Annuities or other types of annuities in the portfolio for which they receive a commission, their base of operations is fee oriented.

The discussion of fees is often a controversial topic. By nature, the investor wants the least amount of fees possible, and the best asset management available. The old saying applies in this instance, "you get what you pay for." If the bottom line is important to you as an investor, which is seeing your accounts grow in value with the least amount of risk possible, then finding an excellent money manager with a proven track record is a key to your success. If your accounts averaged 5-7% a year with a low beta, would you be happy? Probably. So, take a hard look at the style of management, the risk or beta, the history, and then the fees. If you like what you see in the bottom line, which is the return after your fees, you will be pleased over the years. And remember, Column C Red Risk investing is at least a 3 to 5 year window if not longer. Look at managed money in these terms.

In the following pages, I've asked Dan Hunt, the CEO, and Bryce Kommerstad, Chief Investment Strategist of Redhawk Wealth Advisors, Inc. in Minneapolis, Minnesota, to give us their thoughts on the concept of Tactical Investing vs. Strategic (buy and hold) Investing. Dan is not only a good friend, but I must disclose that I am an affiliated Investment Advisor Representative of Redhawk. So, naturally I'm a believer. Please, enjoy Dan and Bryce's comments. They can both be reached at:

Redhawk Wealth Advisors, Inc.
7400 Metro Blvd, Suite 400, Minneapolis, MN 55439, T: 952-835-4295, F: 952-835-0295
Email: dan@redhawkwa.com website: www.redhawkwa.com

"It's Like Sailing a Boat: Tactical Management"

Dan Hunt, CEO Redhawk Wealth Advisors

Tactical (Definition):
"Of or pertaining to a maneuver or plan of action designed as an expedient toward gaining a desired end or temporary advantage."

It's like sailing a boat. If the wind is blowing over the port (left) side of the boat, your sails will be on the starboard (right) side and you will be sailing almost in parallel to the wind direction, hopefully a little downwind to pick up some speed. What if the wind changes direction, literally 180 degrees? When it does, you must tack! You are tactical in your approach to sailing or you: 1) stall, or 2) flip over. We look at how we manage our client's accounts the very same way. That's one big reason we were hired in the first place. Our advisers know it is what happens before the actual management of the assets that is equally important. It is the navigational map and the what-ifs that must be contemplated before ever 'sailing the boat' in the first place.

Is tactical management right, wrong, or indifferent? What would one think to say? If you are doing it, you say it's right. If you are randomly walking down Wall Street in "buy and hope" mode, you are saying it is foolish. If you are in bonds, CDs, and annuities you could be: 1) indifferent, 2) in "I told you so" mode, or 3) looking for the right time to get back in. The primary reason we believe it is right is there is very little chance we will dose at the wheel. In today's volatile market driven in part by what we call, "Insta-mation," that is, instant and infinite information at our fingertips all the time, the markets can move up or down 10% or more very quickly. The response to such moves, however, should have already been contemplated. The worst case scenarios should have already been thought through, or the sailing trip will pose too much risk, will cause reactive decisions that could fail, and simply will not be a fun ride.

All of Redhawk's portfolios share a common theme: they are **Tactical** in their investment management approach. Redhawk is not a promoter of long-term 'buy and hold;' rather, we are a promoter of a long-term 'investment and risk management process.' All of our portfolios utilize Exchange-Traded Funds (ETFs) and follow a strict investment discipline that directs us to "own the strength and avoid the weakness." Furthermore, we strongly believe that the key determinant of long-term performance is overall asset allocation (not individual security selection or market timing). For many years, investors have primarily focused on generating returns by attempting to select the best managers within each broad asset class. However, this approach fails to capitalize on the ability to add potential return by **tactically** allocating between these asset classes. All of Redhawk's strategies attempt to capitalize on the inefficiencies between entire markets, sectors, and countries to ultimately increase return potential and reduce portfolio risk.

"Tactical Asset Management"

Bryce Kommerstad,
Chief Investment Strategist, Redhawk Wealth Advisors

Tactical: 1) small scale actions serving a larger purpose, or 2) adroit in planning or maneuvering to accomplish a purpose. The word tactical has been commonly used going back centuries to describe certain military actions, but has also become widely used in investment circles to describe a type of investment strategy.

Tactical investment strategies allow for more fine tuning, more small moves within the framework of larger strategic goals (i.e., beating the S&P 500 or other benchmarks).

In order for tactical strategies to work well, practitioners must have an in-depth understanding of risk/return. For example, a broad strategy would involve buying and holding the S&P 500 Index. By contrast, a tactical strategy using the S&P 500 as its benchmark might look at the "style components" making up the S&P 500—Large Growth and Large Value—and determine from a risk/return perspective which one is best to own during a given period, when to switch, or even when to own both. The goal of the tactical strategy is to reduce risk and improve return versus simply holding the Index.

A growing understanding through the years of the asset classes reflecting *systematic risk* (risk of being in the market, can't be diversified away), and the emergence of efficient investment vehicles reflecting these asset classes, have combined to fuel the growth of tactical investment management strategies.

Generally speaking, strategic investment strategies involve buying and holding broad stock indexes like the S&P 500 and EAFE (international developed market index), and/or broad bond indexes like the Barclays US Aggregate Index. Tactical strategies tend to drill deeper and focus on the component parts of these indexes, investing in the strong components and avoiding the weak ones. A tactical manager would argue, 'why hold the strong and the weak when you can hold just the strong?'

The key to success in tactical investment management is the ability to identify component parts of broad indexes with regular, predictable wide differences in performance during specific time frames. This offers an opportunity to own the better performers and avoid the poor performers during those periods. Examples of these component parts would be equity asset classes defined by Style, Size, Sectors, Countries, and Global Regions. Bond components would be asset classes defined by type, maturity, rating, and geography.

Redhawk's own Global Tactical Asset Allocation strategy:

Redhawk Global TAA Strategy

- The Global TAA Strategy utilizes three active strategies (Style, Sector, International), Broad Market Indexes (i.e., S&P 500, EAFE), a Real Estate Index, a Commodity Index, and Cash. A quantitatively driven system is employed to allocate and reallocate among these components as market opportunities and risks change over time (i.e., Growth or Value? Large Cap or Small Cap? US or International? Emerging or Developed? Own Commodities / Real Estate, or not?)
- At the heart of our three active equity strategies is the identification of powerful, regularly recurring market opportunities associated with the investment "categories" that underlie each strategy.

• **Style** Categories: Large Growth, Small Value, Mid Growth, etc.
Sector Categories: Healthcare, Technology, Energy, etc.
International Categories: Germany, Singapore, Brazil, etc.

• Investment opportunities are created by consistent **wide performance spreads** and regular **rotation in leadership** that exist among the categories within each strategy.

• The average annual **performance spread** between the best and worst performing **Style** categories is approximately 20%. It's even greater among **Sector** categories and greater still among **International** categories.

• There's also regular **rotation in leadership**. Example: **Style** rotation (and wide performance spreads!) is vividly illustrated by comparing the returns of two Style categories, Large Growth and Small Value, during the years 1998 – 2001:

	1998	**1999**	**2000**	**2001**
Large Growth	**+42**	**+28**	**-22**	**-13**
Small Value	**-5**	**+3**	**+20**	**+13**

• Proper analysis of the critically important information above provides a great opportunity to generate superior returns and, at the same time, control risk. We focus on relative strength among the investment categories within our Style, Sector, and International Strategies.

• Our analysis of investment opportunities is done through a proprietary, quantitative methodology, which directs us to buy the strength and avoid the weakness. Purchases are made via low cost exchange traded funds (ETFs) that mirror the investment categories we follow.

The objective of the Global TAA Strategy is to outperform the S&P 500 Index over any 5-year period of time.

Tactical asset allocation was given its academic underpinnings by the groundbreaking research of Nobel Prize winner William F. Sharpe. He showed that 90% of risk/return in US equities could be explained by Style & Size (Growth/Value, Large/Small). Excerpts from an article we wrote some years ago concerning Sharpe and his research follows:

"In the late 1980's and early 1990's, one of the leading thinkers in the U.S. changed the face of investing forever. For his efforts, William F. Sharpe was awarded the Nobel Prize in Financial Economics. Sharpe's breakthrough thinking allowed investment practitioners to view the "systematic" elements of the equity market from a "style" driven perspective. Style was originally defined around the price-to-book and cap size relationships of equities, and has been somewhat expanded beyond that in recent years.

For the first time, U.S. plan sponsors, consultants, and money managers had a credible way of getting their arms around the unlimited complexities of risk and return. Sharpe was joined by University of Chicago academics, Fama and French, in identifying price-to-book and capitalization size as the most important drivers of systematic return in stocks. Sharpe's work, however, went much further than Fama and French - it gave us the wisdom to understand that ***style actually dominates stock selection.***

Previously, consultants and money managers strongly believed that stock selection was the key determinant of excess returns. This investment belief was held for decades until Sharpe's work revealed the elegant simplicity of "style" as the basis for understanding the footprints of risk and return in the securities markets.

Modern Portfolio Theory was given a deeper systematic underpinning as it became clear that style cycles existed and rotated over one to four year time periods, and could be evaluated with disciplines driven by economic, valuation, fundamental, interest rate, and price behavior existing at the style level of risk and return. From plan sponsor and consulting backgrounds, we observed first-hand the regular in-favor and out-of-favor rotations of money managers in accord with their style discipline. Style cycles going back to the early 70's were exhaustively studied and distinct style periods were identified. In addition, reliable style data reaching as far back as 1926 now provides a base for identifying growth and value cycles over eight decades of U.S. investment history. Style leadership became the predominant way to understand the most in-favor investment style, whether growth or value. Proprietary investment disciplines were built to identify and exploit the style cyclical nature of investment returns over multiple years of time. Suddenly, the plan sponsor world, the academic world, and the money management world were all on the same course of applied style management as one of the most comprehensive ways of establishing aggregate risk control, and for capturing significant style-driven returns in the U.S equity market."

Disclaimer: *Certain statements contained herein may be statements of future expectations and other forward-looking statements that are based on management's current views and assumptions and involve known and unknown risks and uncertainties that could cause actual results, performance or events to differ materially from those expressed or implied in such statements. In addition to statements which are forward-looking by reason of context, the words 'may, will, should, expects, plans, intends, anticipates, believes, estimates, predicts, potential, or continue' and similar expressions identify forward-looking statements.*

Actual results, performance or events may differ materially from those in such statements due to, without limitation, (i) actual research performance, (ii) management expense ratios, (iii) size of market opportunity, (iv) changing levels of competition, (v) changes in laws and regulations, (vi) changes in process technologies, (vii) the impact of acquisitions, including related integration issues, (viii) reorganization measures, (ix) general competitive factors on a local, regional, national and/or global basis (x) and, financial projections. Many of these factors may be more likely to occur, or more pronounced, as a result of terrorist activities and their consequences.

The matters discussed herein may also involve risks and uncertainties. The company assumes no obligation to update any forward-looking information contained herein, and assumes no liability for the accuracy of any of the information presented herein as of a future date.

- Appendix Five -

Endnotes

Chapter One

1. "What does risk mean?" Investopedia.com. 8 June 2010. <http://www.investopedia.com/terms/r/risk.asp>..
2. United States. Board of Governors Federal Reserve System. Instrument, "CDs (secondary market)", Maturity, "6-month". 6 June 2010 <http://www.federalreserve.gov/releases/h15/data/Annual/H15_CD_M6.txt>.

Chapter Two

1. YahooFinance.com. 11 August 2010. Dow Interactive Chart from 2000-2009. 11 August 2010. <http://finance.yahoo.com>.
2. "Invest". Merriam-Webster.com. 12 August 2010.. Merriam-Webster Online Dictionary, 2009. 12 August 2010 <http://www.merriam-webster.com/dictionary/invest>.
3. "Gamble". Merriam-Webster.com. 12 August 2010.. Merriam-Webster Online Dictionary, 2009. 12 August 2010 <http://www.merriam-webster.com/dictionary/gamble>.
4. Edward Winslow. Blind Faith. San Francisco: Berrett-Koehler Publishers, Inc., 2003
5. Edward Winslow. Blind Faith. San Francisco: Berrett-Koehler Publishers, Inc., 2003
6. "History of 401(k) Plans", Employee Benefit Research Institute, February 2005.

7. Investment Company Institute. The US Retirement Market 2007. Research Fundamentals. Vol. 17, No. 3. 2008.
8. "Dow Jones Industrial Average History". Dow Jones Indexes. <http://www.djindexes.com/djia2008/docs/djia-historical-components.pdf>. September 4, 2010
9. Russell Napier. The Anatomy of a Bear. Great Britain: Harriman House, Ltd., 2009
10. Russell Napier. The Anatomy of a Bear. Great Britain: Harriman House, Ltd., 2009

Chapter Three

1. "Funny Stockbroker Jokes" Workjoke.com. August 7, 2010. <http://www.workjoke.com/stockbrokers-jokes.html#739>.
2. "Wire House Broker" Investopedia.com. April 2009. <http://www.investopedia.com/terms/w/wire-house-broker.asp>.
3. "Warren Buffet Quotes" brainyquote.com, September 14, 2010.<http://www.brainyquote.com/quotes/authors/w/warren_buffett_3.html>.
4. Weininger, Bruce, CPA, CFP. "Euthanize Wealth Management Practices" Investment Advisor Magazine. July 2009: 68
5. Stein, Ben. "Lessons from a Very Bad Year." YahooFinance.com/Personal Finance. 22 Dec. 2008. <http://finance.yahoo.com/expert/article/yourlife/130751>.
6. YahooFinance.com. 22 Aug. 2010. S&P 500 Interactive Chart from 200-2009. <http://finance.yahoo.com>.
7. Cochrane, Tom. "An Interview with Wharton Professor David Babbel – Part One." AnnuityDigest.com, 26 July 2009. <http://www.annuitydigest.com/blog/tom/interview-wharton-professor-david-babbel-part-one>.
8. Babbel, David F. "Un-supermodels and the FIA." Ibbotson Associates/IFID Centre Conference, University of Chicago – Gleacher Center. Guaranteed Living Income Benefit Insurance Products. November 11, 2008

Chapter Four

1. Samuelson, William, Boston University and Zeckhauser, Richard, Harvard University. “Status Quo Bias in Decision Making.” Journal of Risk and Uncertainty. 1:7-59 (1988) Kluwer Academic Publishers, Boston
2. Elzweig, Mark. “Slash and Burn: The New Wall Street Growth Model” 8 Nov. 2009. Investment News.com. <http://www.investmentnews.com/apps/pbcs.dll/article?AID=/20091108/REG/311089985>.

Chapter Five

1. United States. Board of Governors Federal Reserve System. Instrument, “CDs (secondary market)”, Maturity, “6-month”. 6 June 2010 <http://www.federalreserve.gov/releases/h15/data/Annual/H15_CD_M6.txt>.
2. “Current Annual Inflation Rate.” Inflationdata.com. 16 Sept. 2010. Capital Professional Services, LLC. <http://inflationdata.com/Inflation/Inflation_Rate/CurrentInflation.asp>.
3. “Annuities Double CD Performance.” InsuranceNewsnet Magazine. December 2008: 24.
4. YahooFinance.com. 14 Sept. 2010. S&P 500 Interactive Chart from 1995-1999. <http://finance.yahoo.com>.

Chapter Six

1. United States. Board of Governors Federal Reserve System. Instrument, “CDs (secondary market)”, Maturity, “6-month”. 6 June 2010

Chapter Seven

1. “Dennis Green Meltdown.” YouTube.com. 26 Oct. 2006. <http://www.youtube.com/watch?v=m_N1OjGhIFc>.

Chapter Eight

1. “Systematic Risk.” Investopedia.com. 16 Sept. 2010. <http://www.investopedia.com/terms/s/systematicrisk.asp>.
2. “Standard Deviation” Investopedia.com. 16 Sept. 2010. <http://www.investopedia.com/terms/s/standarddeviation.asp>.

3. "R-Squared." Investopedia.com. 16 Sept. 2010. <http://www.investopedia.com/terms/r/r-squared.asp>.
4. YahooFinance.com. 22 Aug. 2010. CGM Focus Fund Performance. <http://finance.yahoo.com/q/pm?s=CGMFX+Performance>.
5. YahooFinance.com. 22 Aug. 2010. AGTHX Performance. <http://finance.yahoo.com/q/pm?s=AGTHX+Performance>.

Chapter Nine

1. "Bear Market." Investopedia.com. 16 Sept. 2010. <http://www.investopedia.com/terms/b/bearmarket.asp>.
2. Russell Napier. The Anatomy of a Bear. Great Britain: Harriman House, Ltd., 2009
3. "John D. Rockefeller Quotes." thinkexist.com. 22 Aug. 2010. John D. Rockefeller American Industrialist and philanthropist, founder of the Standard Oil Company, 1839-1937. <http://thinkexist.com/quotes/john_d._rockefeller/2.html>.
4. "Warren Buffett Quotes." BrainyQuote.com. 17 Sept. 2010. <http://www.brainyquote.com/quotes/authors/w/warren_buffett_2.html>.
5. Russell Napier. The Anatomy of a Bear. Great Britain: Harriman House, Ltd., 2009
6. YahooFinance.com. 22 Aug. 2010. S&P 500 Interactive Chart from 1995-1999. <http://finance.yahoo.com>.
7. Ibid.
8. "Warren Buffett Quotes." BrainyQuote.com, 17 Sept. 2010. <http://www.brainyquote.com/quotes/authors/w/warren_buffett_2.html>.

Chapter Ten

1. "What is the Average Retirement Age?" WiseGeek.com. 20 Sept. 2010. <http://www.wisegeek.com/what-is-the-average-retirement-age.htm>.
2. United States. Social Security Online. Period Life Table – Actuarial Publications. <http://www.ssa.gov/OACT/STATS/table4c6.html>.

3. YahooFinance.com. 20 Sept. 2010. S&P 500 Interactive Chart from 1995-1999. <http://finance.yahoo.com>.

Chapter Eleven

1. "History of 401(k) Plans: An Update, Facts from EBRI." EBRI.org. Feb. 2009. Employee Benefit Research Institute. 17 Aug. 2010. <http://www.ebri.org/pdf/publications/facts/0205fact.a.pdf >.
2. "The U.S. Retirement Market, 2007." ICI.org. Investment Company Institute. Research Fundamentals. July 2008. Vol. 17 No. 3A. < http://www.ici.org/pdf/fm-v17n3_appendix.pdf>.
3. United States. Internal Revenue Service. Department of the Treasury. EP Compliance Risk Assessments – 401(k) Plans. March 4, 2009. <http://www.irs.gov/retirement/article/0,,id=147172,00.html>.
4. Ibid.
5. Choate,Natalie. "Life and Deat Planning for Retirement Benefits: Sixth Edition, completely revised." Boston. Ataxplan Publications:2006.
6. Ibid.
7. Ibid.
8. Ibid.
9. Ibid.
10. Ebeling, Ashlea. "The Great 401(k) Escape." Forbes.com. 31 Jan. 2008. <http://www.forbes.com/forbes/2008/0225/046.html>.

Chapter Twelve

1. "Sir Edmund Hillary Biography: Conqueror of Mt. Everest." Achievement.org. Academy of Achievement. 10 Jan. 2008. <http://www.achievement.org/autodoc/page/hil0pro-1>.
2. Clark, Leisl and Salkeld, Audrey. "The Mystery of Mallory and Irvine '24" PBS.org. Nov. 2000. NOVA Online Adventure. 19 Aug. 2010. <http://www.pbs.org/wgbh/nova/everest/lost/mystery/>.

3. Templeton, Tim. The Referral of a Lifetime. San Francisco. Berrett-Koehler Publishers. 2003-2004
4. Ibid.
5. Taylor, Don A. and Worsham, C. Bruce. Financial Planning: Process and Environment. Bryn Mawr: The American College. 2007

Chapter Thirteen

1. Marion, Jack. Change Buyer Behavior and Sell More Annuities. Indexannuity.org. 2009 <http://www.indexannuity.org/Change%20Buyer%20Behavior%20(excerpts).pdf>
2. "Bias." Dictionary.com, 22 Sept. 2010. <http://dictionary.reference.com/browse/bias>.
3. Rogers, John W., Jr. "Emotional Investing." Forbes.com. The Patient Investor. 31 Oct. 2005. <http://www.forbes.com/forbes/2005/1031/218.html>.
4. Myers, Daniel, CFA. Buy When There's Blood in the Streets. Investopedia.com. 22 Sept. 2010. <http://www.investopedia.com/articles/financial-theory/08/contrarian-investing.asp>.

Chapter Fourteen

No Footnotes